The Autobiography of Jesus

PARK CITY BAPTIST CHURCH
PARK CITY, KENTUCKY.

The Autobiography of Jesus

What He Said About Himself

Leslie D. Weatherhead

ABINGDON

Nashville

THE AUTOBIOGRAPHY OF JESUS
A Festival Book

ISBN: 0-687-02318-1

Festival edition published May 1980

Printed in the United States of America

This book is affectionately dedicated to my friend

THE LATE

O. DICKINSON STREET, SR.

and to his son and daughter-in-law
DICK and GRACE ANN

as a small recognition of
all they did to make my
American visit such a
happy experience

Preface

NOTHING is more important than what I call "looking at Jesus." If we take the sentences in which he says, "I am," then we are looking at his own portraits of himself. It is as though we studied an autobiography which he had signed himself. And "looking at Jesus" is not just the idle act of a quiet hour on the part of a pietistic recluse. We can never see him without being challenged to extend our service to the world and correct our sense of values, and without being empowered to alter our lives. If he is, as I believe, the Son of God, the clearest and highest revelation of God's nature and purpose, then he is supremely relevant to all of us today and to all phases of our life together. To pretend he does not exist is only to postpone an inevitable encounter, for he waits at the end of every road man can take. To move away from him is chaos and disaster, whether we speak individually, industrially, socially, politically, or internationally. To move toward him is to follow the path of personal integration and world peace.

A critic of these studies might well protest that I have accepted too easily the reliability of the evangelists' testimony. "How do you know," he might ask, "that we can depend on accurate reporting? No shorthand notes were taken, and biased reporting is notorious. If the writer wanted to 'sell' certain ideas about Christ, how easily he could do so! May not the Gospels be illustrations of sheer propanganda?"

I would reply by reminding such a critic than an Eastern Jewish memory was a far more reliable

THE AUTOBIOGRAPHY OF JESUS

instrument than a Western modern one. For instance, one reads that every Jew knew the psalms by heart and many passages of the Law as well. Now, with our fountain pens and notebooks ready, we do not depend on memory and so its powers have diminished. In our Lord's day, spoken words would be remembered with far greater accuracy than they would today.

It is granted that in the Fourth Gospel, from which many passages in this book are taken, we have the meditations of a devout mind rather than the actual words of Jesus. But the meditations were based on the words, and "the clear statements recorded in the Fourth Gospel are supported by the very earliest records of His teaching that we possess."[1] Further, who among all the sons of men is likely to have invented such sayings as these?

One friendly critic of these lectures wrote me that he suspected the Gospel writers of "trying to sell the idea of a divine Christ," but that to worship a man would be to a devout Jew the most blasphemous heresy possible. That the early Church, so largely constructed of Jews, should within such a short period after his death, ask the world to believe that Jesus had risen and was a divine being, the Son of God at the right hand of God the Father, is incredible save by accepting the evidence that Jesus acted and spoke more or less as the Gospels report. So often the Gospel narratives amaze one by what they include as well as by what they omit. They include matter which a "cooked account" would omit. Men writing to "sell the idea of a divine Christ" would write stories like the apocryphal Gospel of Thomas which the early Church rejected, and they would never have admitted, for example, that Jesus was tired (John 4:6), or hungry (Matt. 4:2; Luke 4:2; Matt. 21:18; Mark 11:12), or that there

[1]Principal Frederic Greeves in *An Approach to Christian Doctrine*.

were things he did not know (Matt. 24:36), or that he could be surprised (Matt. 8:10). Omniscience knows no surprises. Omnipotence is never tired and surely need never be hungry.

I earnestly hope I have not obscured or distorted the picture of the Master, but that what I have written may be found to set forth, in all its winsome appeal and majestic bearing, the Gospel picture of him who spake as never man spake and who made clear, at one and the same time, God's idea of man and man's idea of God.

What follows grew out of some lectures which I delivered in 1954 at the First Methodist Church, Wichita Falls, Texas. These lectures are financed by a lifelong Methodist, Joseph J. Perkins, and I was privileged to be the first British minister to deliver them. I gathered that although the word "lectures" was generously used, what was wanted each time was really a long sermon. At any rate, that was what I "delivered." And since one of my besetting sins is to preach too long, it was wonderful to be allotted an hour for each talk. One wonders what size audiences one would have in a smallish town in England if the same arrangements were made. I was amazed and delighted to find that even on the weekday mornings, one could be sure of fifteen hundred people and in the evenings, sometimes over two thousand. I have written these talks all out again for this volume and added scripture references, the study of which would make the book more valuable.

I shall never forget the kindness shown to me at Wichita Falls by the very able minister, Dr. Alfred H. Freeman, and his charming wife; by Mr. and Mrs. Perkins; by Dr. Dorbantz, who saw me through a difficult patch in the matter of health; by Mr. and Mrs. O. Dickinson Street, Jr., who, having returned to New York, flew fifteen hundred miles to be with me again and to hear the lectures; and by my beloved friend and tour-manager, Mr. Harry Fish, who was like a brother to me for nearly four months.

A further word of deep thankfulness goes to my wife; my colleague, the Rev. Herbert T. Lewis, M.A.; and my secretary, Miss Winifred Haddon, who have given me unstinted help in preparing these talks for publication. I should like to close my Preface with some words of Dr. John Hunter which are constantly my own prayer:

Dear Master, in Whose Life I see
All that I long and fail to be,
Let Thy clear light for ever shine,
To shame and guide this life of mine.

Though what I dream and what I do
In my poor days are always two,
Help me, oppressed by things undone,
O Thou, Whose dreams and deeds were one.

LESLIE D. WEATHERHEAD

The City Temple, London

Contents

I

The Bread of Life

Jesus said unto them, I am the bread of life. —JOHN 6:35

WHEN we read through the sixth chapter of John's Gospel, I think we must feel great sympathy for those who, hearing its message for the first time, found it difficult. Indeed, it is difficult for us today. Listen!

I am the living bread which came down out of heaven: if any man eat of this bread, he shall live for ever: yea and the bread which I will give is my flesh, for the life of the world. (vs. 51)

And again:

Except ye eat the flesh of the Son of man and drink his blood, ye have not life in yourselves. He that eateth my flesh and drinketh my blood hath eternal life; and I will raise him up at the last day. For my flesh is meat indeed, and my blood is drink indeed. He that eateth my flesh and drinketh my blood abideth in me, and I in him. (vss. 53-56)

Finally, even more bluntly still, we come across this sentence: "He that eateth me, he also shall live because of me" (vs. 57).

What *are* we to make of such language? I have preached in Fiji to men who can remember the cannibalistic orgies of only two generations ago. I wonder what some of the older Fijian Christians made of these words when they heard them first. It is no wonder that the Jews angrily asked: "How can this man give us his flesh to eat?" (vs. 52).

"Is not this Jesus, the son of Joseph, whose father and mother we know? how doth he now say, I come down out of heaven?" (vs. 42).

Many even of the disciples said: "This is a hard saying; who can hear it?" Jesus frequently seems to have assessed human intelligence higher than the facts justified. He seemed surprised on this occasion that his hearers found the words difficult. "Doth this cause you to stumble?" he asked. We can almost see, in imagination, their puzzled, angry faces; angry because they were so puzzled. Imaginatively one can almost hear a man saying: "Well, I give it up. With all the good will in the world what can you make of such words?" And reading on through the chapter we come to the sad verse: "Upon this many of his disciples went back, and walked no more with him" (vs. 66). And the following verse sounds to me as sad as any in the Gospels: "Jesus said therefore unto the twelve, Would ye also go away?" Peter—thank God for Peter!—relieves the painful tension by his simple and sublime reply: "Lord, to whom shall we go? thou hast the words of eternal life. And we have believed and know that thou art the Holy One of God" (vss. 68-69). It is as though he said: "We don't pretend to understand you, but we have seen too much to desert you. We believe in you however puzzled we may be over what you say. We have seen God in you as in no one else. You have the words of eternal life. We cannot find them anywhere else. We won't leave you for there is nowhere else to go."

So, I suppose, Peter and the others would put Christ's words away in their minds as one might put into a drawer a letter from a dear friend who wrote in a foreign language which one could not understand, to take it out when an interpreter turned up who could reveal its meaning. The Spirit of Truth was promised to them and he is promised to us. "He taketh of mine," said Jesus, "and shall declare it unto you. He shall guide you into all the truth." We, too, are dull and slow, but there are at least some things we can be shown.

> Thou canst make me understand,
> Though I am slow of heart.

The general purpose of this message of Jesus seems to me to be that God is as necessary to the fullest and truest—that is the spiritual—life of man as bread is necessary to the life of his body, and that because Jesus himself can supply that need, he is indeed the Bread of Life. Let us at the very beginning try to put aside repellent and cannibal ideas, and use the word "eat" to mean that we take within ourselves something from without ourselves. Then even the sentence that seems crudest of all will light up with meaning. "He that eateth me . . . shall live because of me."

Let us first make the obvious but very important point that *life depends on God-given bread.*

All bread is God-given. It is sent down from heaven giving life into the world. Without God's gifts of grain and sunshine and rain, there would be no cornfields. Yet without man's labor, there would be no bread. Here we have an illustration of Augustine's pregnant saying: "Without God, we cannot; without us, God will not." I don't think I know a saying which contains more wisdom in fewer words than this. Without God we cannot make a loaf. Without us God will not make a loaf. To the man of insight a loaf is a symbol of that necessary cooperation of God with man, for which, so often, God waits while man wonders why God does not act by "sheer omnipotence." We must not take time to go into it fully now, but Augustine's word is a key that unlocks a thousand doors for those who in so many situations—illness, for instance—ask why God doesn't do this and that. The

THE AUTOBIOGRAPHY OF JESUS

answer often is that he waits for man's cooperation, a cooperation which asks from man knowledge and skill. If God overrode man's contribution by what people call sheer omnipotence, man would never learn anything. So God puts coal in the hills, but he will not make a fire, and he grows the corn in our cornfields, but he will not make a loaf.

> Back of the loaf is the snowy flour,
> Back of the flour, the mill;
> Back of the mill are the wheat and the shower
> And the sun and the Father's will.

We see, then, that a loaf of bread is a symbol of our utter dependence on God, of our utter dependence on bread, and, in this form of society in which we live, of our utter dependence on those who make our bread for us. Those of us who live a very busy life might pause to remember that bread is so essential that unless some of us were farmers and millers all the time, all of us would have to be farmers and millers part of the time, for bread we must have.

A few invalids and ascetics excepted, every man in the world will eat bread—or its Eastern equivalent, rice—today. Food was the most primitive need of primitive man in primitive days. To produce it was the first requirement of man's labor. To obtain it was probably the first object of man's prayer. To hoard wheat was probably the first sign of human wealth. To distribute it to the needy was probably the first act of human benevolence. More than three thousand years ago Moses instructed the Jewish farmers to leave the corners of the wheatfield unharvested so that the poor might reap there (Lev. 19:9). The first expression of human fellowship was the sharing of a meal. Yet the highest expression of the highest faculty in the highest religion of the world is to eat bread together. The supreme act of Christian devotion and dedication is to eat bread in the sacrament of Holy Communion, in which we "feed in our hearts by faith with thanksgiving" on the Bread of Life. Amid the many symbolic meanings of that great sacrament is this: that as bread is necessary to the life of the body, the receiving of God into ourselves is necessary to the life of the soul.

Eating bread has always linked man with God, though man does not always remember this. Curiously enough the Oxyrhynchus Papyri contain an invitation from one man to another to eat at the table of the god Serapis, the corn-god. Both the invited guest and the person inviting him thought of themselves as fellow guests at the table of the Lord Serapis who was the host of both. Anything done in the presence of the god was binding, and from time immemorial eating bread together has had a divine significance. It was because bread was eaten in the presence of the god that to eat with a person forged a link of friendship with him. One must not eat with the god and then fight one's fellow guest. Indeed, men offered meat to God that they might eat with him and thus become friends with him, obtaining thereby his friendship and protection. Here, some think, is the beginning of the practice of offering a sacrifice.

A recent experience showed me very clearly how essential to life is bread. I stood in the balcony of a hall used for the physical training of young men. There must have been twenty of them who, wisely enough, devoted a couple of spare evenings a week to what is called physical culture. They were members of a health club. They did the most difficult physical exercises, guaranteed by their ingenious inventor to bring into play during the evening every muscle of their bodies. After this, to cool down, they listened to talks on diet, on hygiene, on the value of sunlight and fresh air and proper hours of sleep. After

17

the lecture they adjourned to a swimming pool in the same building and learned how to dive and float and save life. I did not watch them do so, but I am quite sure they would all go home—and eat! Imagine the comment of the gym instructor if I had said to him: "I thought *you* could make men strong. Why do they need to go and eat?"

Has the significance of this fact dawned on us that while, up to a point, exercise and fresh air spell health, to exercise without eating will rapidly make us weaker, not stronger? Men who train for a strenuous boat race not only pay attention to exercise, but to food. I don't suppose many realize it, but because of this fact they all pay tribute to their need of God, for tell me one food that does not ultimately come from God.

If, therefore, physical life depends on bread, on our receiving into ourselves something that comes from God, is it likely that the other parts of man's nature—his mind and his spirit—can really *live* without any help from outside?

So we come to our second point: *life in any but its most elementary form depends on more than bread.*

Jesus was not blind to man's need of bread. Those who think it is wrong to pray for material things might ponder the fact that in the heart of the model prayer, Jesus placed this petition, "Give us this day our daily bread," or, perhaps the words are better translated: "Give us daily our bread for the coming day" (Matt. 6:11).

In his own poignant temptation in the wilderness, the knowledge of which, since he was alone, must have come to us from himself, it seems unlikely that it was only his own physical hunger he was thinking about. His own beloved people, who moved him to compassion, were in hundreds of cases starving. He so wanted to win their ear and make them understand. But can one preach of a spiritual kingdom to men who are hungry? Would it not be better, hinted the Evil One, to proclaim some "social gospel," to give them bread? Let the poor be fed and then they will listen. It was a keen temptation to a loving spirit. But in his quiet hours of meditation and communion with God, Jesus put it from him. He must not buy men's interest or bribe their loyalty with bread. Christ answered the tempter with one of the most important sentences in the world. "Man shall not *live* by bread alone, but by every word that proceedeth out of the mouth of God" (Matt. 4:4).

Now what does "to live" mean? Does it not mean that the organism must be in harmonious relationship with its relevant environment and with other parts of the related organism? My eyes only really "live" if they are in a harmonious relationship with their relevant environment which is called light. If that relationship is broken on either side, the eye going wrong or light being excluded, the eye "dies." It does not function as a seeing instrument. It does not do that which it was made to do. It is not sensitive, and sensitivity is life. In a sense the eye "eats" light. My ears must be in a harmonious relationship with sound. Sound is their relevant environment. If the sounds which others hear do not reach my ears, then the latter are not "living" in any real sense. My ears must "eat" sound to live. My lungs must "eat" air. And so with other organs of the body.

The life of the mind is not dissimilar. The relevant environment of the mind we could call "the world of true ideas." If a man's mind is not *en rapport* with the world of true ideas at any point, his mind is not fully "living." If, for example, a grocer constantly thinks he is the pope or the king, then his mind is not in a harmonious relationship with truth. It is a faulty instrument. It is not sensitive to truth. We call the condition dis-ease. His mind is not healthily living at all points. Truth is its only healthy diet.

The life of the soul, man's essential self, is not dissimilar. The relevant environment of the soul we call

God. If *all* traffic with God were cut off, man's soul would perish. For in order to "live" it needs to be in a harmonious relationship with God. Of his infinite mercy God has made it very difficult for even a careless man to shut off all contact with Him. Truth, beauty, and goodness appeal to many who conventionally are called —or call themselves—irreligious, and all three are attributes of God. But there is no truer word in the world than that of our Lord when he said: "Man shall not *live* by bread alone." "If thou hast two loaves," said Mohammed, "sell one and buy lilies." For full living we feel we need beauty, and many a man, pretending to be irreligious, nourishes his soul on nature, on poetry, on art, on music, on love, on the truth of mathematics or the goodness of some secret hero, on the moral values which his parents sowed in his mind when he was a child, and—a point to which I shall return—on the friendship of others. It is a figure of speech we do not often use, but it would be true to say man eats these things.

For instance, a father tells me that his daughter "simply *devours*" poetry. Please note the italicized word. Richard Pape, in his book *Boldness Be My Friend,* speaking of the fighting soldiers in the last war, stressed the importance to them of the loyalty of their womenfolk. He writes: "Any unfaithfulness of women back at home made men rapidly deteriorate. . . . The love for a wife or a sweetheart . . . *was the food that fed their hearts.*"[1] A friend of mine one day, searching for accommodation, said to me: "I must have room for my piano." Knowing him well, I find no exaggeration in the phrase that he "feeds" on music. Have you not heard of anyone of whom one could say, "She would be lost without her music"? For myself I like a diet of mountains! I eat them! I mean, of course, that there is something about them on which I can feed a spirit

[1] Italics mine.

starved in London Town. When I can spend a day among them, something from them enters my being and feeds it with peace and quietude.

We can understand Masefield in the lovely poem "Sea Fever," crying:

I must go down to the seas again, for the call of the running tide
Is a wild call and a clear call that may not be denied.[2]

If it "may not be denied," we are not exaggerating when we use the word "hunger" as its synonym.

So W. B. Yeats, the poet, feels he must arise and go to Innisfree. Standing on the gray pavements he can feel the hunger in "the deep heart's core." He craves for the beauty and peace of his magic island.

And I shall have some peace there, for peace comes dropping slow,
Dropping from the veils of the morning to where the cricket sings;
There midnight's all a-glimmer, and noon a purple glow,
And evening full of the linnet's wings.[3]

Man feeds and satisfies and nourishes an essential part of his nature not on bread alone, but on *other expressions of God's meanings*. You see a "word" is an expression of meaning. Mountains express God's meaning, so do lilies and so do birds, so does beautiful music, so does kindness, and so does love. They are all words of God because they all express his meaning. There is no truer sentence in the world than this: "Man

---

[2]*Collected Poems*. Copyright 1953 by The Macmillan Company. Used by permission.

[3]"The Lake Isle of Innisfree," from *The Collected Poems of W. B. Yeats*. Copyright 1950 by The Macmillan Company. Used by permission.

shall not live by bread alone, but by *every word* that proceedeth out of the mouth of God."

So quite simply we come to the Word made flesh. In the sense in which I have been using the word "eat," this Man *has* given us his flesh to eat. It is his human nature that means so much to us. His life in the flesh reveals a supreme meaning of God. It is a Word translated into flesh, and because we must take it into ourselves, just as we feed on music, it is indeed the Bread of Life which came down from heaven. We must "eat" him.

I know that some of the expressions, both in the sixth chapter of John and in our Prayer Book, sometimes repel us. I am hoping that some things said in this chapter may take the repulsion away; for when we say, "Grant us, gracious Lord, so to eat His flesh and to drink His blood," what is meant is that fullness of living demands that the very nature of God must somehow be absorbed by our own nature. For just as the body needs food for its strength and the mind needs food for its buoyancy, so the soul needs food, and the food of the soul is God.

But how can the soul "eat" God? How can God be received into the tiny soul of man? It is here that Jesus comes to us with his revelation of himself as the Bread of Life. He says in the language which shocked his hearers, that we must eat him, feed on him, receive what he is into our very system. "He that eateth me . . . shall live because of me." Clearly, apart from him, God is so vast, so utterly beyond us that to seek to feed on God would be like putting a tiny child down in a cornfield and saying to him: "There is food all round you. Get on with it." The food is not assimilable. It must be translated into a form suitable to the baby. So my tiny baby soul confronts the infinite vastness of God and is as overwhelmed and perplexed as an infant would be in a cornfield. In his loving mercy, therefore, God became compassable. "He *came down* out of heaven." Here is God in a form that I can understand. Here is a Word of poetry that I can devour. Here is the Bread of Life on whom I can nourish my immature and undeveloped spirit.

You may ask: "But how do we feed on Jesus?" Lovers, I am sure, need no expository notes at this point. They can spend hours together practically in silence and their natures are feeding the one on the other in terms of fellowship, friendship, love, support, and so on.

Have you never come home after some exhausting experience feeling spent and weary? Food and sleep play their part in refreshment of the body. Music and poetry can add to the refreshment of the mind. But if you had been solitary and alone you would not have recovered your poise and buoyancy so fully. Husband or wife, lover or friend, provided solicitude, sympathy, understanding. They built up the depleted faith in ourselves which we may have lost for the time being. I will not say that you "eat" your friend, but in the sense we have been using the word, that is what it comes to.

Frankly, I am selfishly glad that my wife does not go about addressing meetings. When I come in at the end of the day from my work, I like her to be *there*. I know I could get a meal at a restaurant and I could get music from the radio. I could get intellectual food from a book, but what I hunger for is her companionship and love.

Now, to me, the very heart of the Christian religion is that Christ offers his friendship, and through that we feed our souls on God. Christ brings life in a new and fuller sense. He is what bread is to the body, what light is to the eyes. Can the body find strength by exercise if food be denied? Can the eyes be made to see by being massaged if light be denied? Can the soul truly live by its own will power and good resolutions, without any help from heaven?

With a friend I came away recently from a home, and when we got down the street, my friend said: "It's like coming away from a tomb, isn't it?" I know exactly what he meant. They were all dead! One would have given anything to be able to impart to them the *joie de vivre*, the joy of living which Christ can bring. The people in the house referred to were quite respectable citizens. They even went to church sometimes. They reminded me of dull, heavy oxen plowing a muddy field uphill on a gray and rainy day! There was no light in their eyes, no joy in their voices. They were dead.

When Jesus said, "Let the dead bury their dead," it sounds a hard saying, but I think the situation may well have been this. A man listened to Jesus and got a glimpse of the new life that he offered. But the man's father was old (his father was not dead because in the East the dead are buried by sunset), and he said to Jesus: "I would like to follow you, but I think I had better wait until my father passes away and I have put things in order at home." And Jesus, who knew how dead the other people in the family were and how this man must be made to follow the light he had seen, said to him: "Leave the other dead people in your family to bury the dead. Now you have seen a glimmer of light, you come with me and find what life is meant to be like." It has been well said that

the tragedy of life is not in the fact of death itself. The tragedy of life is in what dies inside a man while he lives—the death of genuine feeing, the death of inspired response, the death of the awareness that makes it possible to feel in oneself the pain or the glory of other men.

Jesus says he can give us life. He said indeed that he was the Bread of Life, the God-given essential of life. He was so eager to give us that Bread and he knew so well that *bread must be broken before its strength can be imparted,* that he went to Calvary so that broken Bread, assimilable for all, might be at our disposal.

No wonder, still only half-understanding, they cried: "Lord, evermore give us this bread" (John 6:34).

> Ever may my soul be fed
> With this true and living bread;
> Day by day with strength supplied
> Through the life of Him who died.

"I am the Bread of Life," said Jesus. "He that cometh to me shall *never* hunger" (K.J.V.). It is the strongest negative of which the Greek language is capable. We all want energy, power, strength, fullness of life. We are compelled to remember the needs of the body. Our modern culture offers us in variety the foods of the mind. Can it be possible that in our search for life we have forgotten the most fundamental need of all, whose name is God?

I hope all this does not make the gospel sound difficult. My friend, Tom Dring, tells the story of a copy of John's Gospel which came into the possession of a passenger on an Indian train. When he realized that it was part of the Christian Scriptures he became angry, tore it into small pieces and threw it out of the window. But a gang of platelayers was working on the railway line. One of them picked up a tiny fragment and read in his own language just three words: "Bread of Life." Deeply impressed he repeated them aloud. "That is just what I need," he said. "Where can I get it?" Though warned that the phrase was from a Christian book which would contaminate him, he was insistent. He found at last a little Christian community and through its simple forms of worship he found the Christ himself. If a simple Indian coolie could find a new quality of life thus, then, however hard our intellectual problems may be, so that the mind asks continually for more and still more food, the heart's hunger can be satisfied and the soul can find her rest.

Jesus said: "I am the Bread of Life. He that cometh to me shall *never* hunger, never again wander aimlessly not knowing where to look or which way to turn for satisfaction."

II

The True Vine

[Jesus said,] I am the true vine. . . . Abide in me, and I in you. . . . Apart from me ye can do nothing. If a man abide not in me, he is cast forth as a branch, and is withered; and they gather them, and cast them into the fire, and they are burned. . . . Even as the Father hath loved me, I also have loved you: abide ye in my love.
—JOHN 15:1-19

IN this chapter we are to think of Jesus as the True Vine. The word "true" there, we could translate "real." It is the word a banker might use in explaining the difference between a real five-dollar bill and one that was counterfeit. It is the word a jeweler might use who was explaining the difference between a genuine diamond and a sham. Says Jesus: "I am the Real Vine."

Let us look at the scene. Jesus and his disciples have just partaken in the Upper Room of that solemn meal which now we call the Last Supper. It is the last night of his earthly life. The time is about half past eleven. They move slowly and sadly through the silent city so ironically called Jerusalem, the City of Peace. They come out on that great open space on which the Temple was built. In imagination, we can watch them in the bright moonlight of the Passover season, crossing the vast square as they approach the great doors of the Temple. Over the doors, exquisitely carved and covered with gold leaf, is the great Vine, the symbol of all Israel, the Divine Community stemming from

Abraham, Isaac, and Jacob. We can imagine the feelings of the disciples as they admire the carving, the lovely big bunches of grapes, the curving branches, some climbing toward the roof, others sweeping low in graceful curves, every leaf, every tiny tendril carved wih matchless skill and care. We can imagine deeper feelings than admiration as they think of the symbolism. The Jews are the chosen race. In spite of Rome they are the chosen people. God will protect the Vine. His promises are for them alone. The thought made them proud, exclusive, and intolerant.

The familiar words, which all Christians know, blind us to what happened next. Jesus, in one sentence, shattered such complacency. "I am the Real Vine and while you are the branches, yet *everyone* who is in the love-relationship with me has the same life flowing through his soul and is incorporate by that love-relationship into the Divine Community. Abide in me and I will abide in you." Thus all who love Christ are members one of another. Said Marcus Aurelius: "If you only say I am a part *(meros)* not a member *(melos)* you do not love men from the bottom of your heart." Christ is the Whole and wholly lives in every part. He did not say, "I am the Trunk." He is the entire Tree. No branch of the true Vine can disparage another branch. No species of *apartheid* can be sanctioned by Christianity.

With one sentence, accompanied, we imagine, with one gesture, Jesus obliterated forever the narrow claim that the Jews, and they alone, were the Divine Community. It is as though Jesus said: "It is not the accident of Jewish blood, it is not nationality, nor historical prestige, nor geographical situation, nor tradition, nor birth; but *anyone* who is in the love-relationship with me is, by that fact, within the Divine Community. It is no good saying: 'We have Abraham to our father.' The *vital* relation is the love-relation. Abide in my love as I abide in the Father's love."

And now the Vine is not symbolized by a carving on the Jewish Temple. The Vine and the branches are found on all shores, under all skies in all nations. Though we often mourn and watch its leaves wither, fall off, and die, yet, taking the whole world, we are watching it grow and spread, and one day, please God, it will cover the earth, for its fruit contains the very lifeblood of God and its leaves are for the healing of the nations.

Let us look at three implications of our Lord's words important for, and relevant to, our life today.

1. Christ's words make Christianity basically different from every other religion, however lofty some of the teachings of other religions may be.

We need to emphasize this point, especially since there are armchair dilettantes who cull pretty words from Aldous Huxley, and other anthologists who quote selected passages from Eastern religious writers but have never worked among the slums of great eastern cities and seen how the teachings of Hinduism, for example, work out in terms of lives lived in complete harmony with those teachings and yet in moral degradation—and this, in my opinion, not lofty esthetic words, comprises the test of the value of any religion. When it is sincerely tried, what fruit does it bear? Hinduism, for example, has many splendid tenets and many noble sons such as Tagore and Gandhi, yet while in the West all evil is a *denial* of our religion, in the East some evil is an expression of religion: temple prostitution, and caste distinctions, for instance.

Look at this implication of our Lord's words. Man, in a real sense, can be vitally related with God *now*, at once. As the life of the stem flows in the farthest tendril, God's life can empower us *now*.

In Eastern religions such a relationship is the goal of

man's own unaided struggle. After he has struggled on alone, perhaps through many incarnations, he may, at last, attain by sheer will power and meritorious self-discipline a unity with God and, in one religion at least, lose his own individuality as a drop of rain is lost in the river. To this nirvana, Buddhism calls its devotees. But Jesus says: "You can be united with me now as truly as the branches with the Vine." Union with God is not the goal of a life cut off from divine aid. It is a help offered now toward that perfect unity which for all religions is *summum bonum* of all existence.

In one of his books the late James Black tells of a dream he had. In this dream he moved among the old temples of ancient Greece. Near one of them he met a priest and began to talk to him. Pointing to some people approaching the temple, the dreamer said to the priest: "I suppose these people honor and love their god." "Honor?" said the priest. "Love? What do you mean? They fear him because he may destroy them, but love . . ." "Even now," said the dreamer, "I shudder at the very memory of my dream, for with a harsh, coarse, horrible cackle of laughter, the priest said: 'Whoever loved a god?' " "But," said the dreamer, "do not these people seek to know the will of the god?" "Will," said the priest, "he does not work by will, but by whim, by caprice. He may smite with illness, curse with barrenness, blight with disaster. No one can know the mind of a god. One may only appease his anger." "But," said the horrified dreamer, "what of sin? Do not these people seek forgiveness?" "Sin," said the priest, "what is sin? Morality is the affair of the State, but the gods care nothing about that. You talk nonsense. The gods are not interested in men, though for their sport they sometimes plague them. The gods live their own lives and we are lucky if their pleasures keep their attention away from us."

Here is Jesus, whom we truly regard as God made into man, man filled as full of God as man can be without his true humanity being destroyed, saying that we may abide in him by loving him and doing his will and that through us his life will flow and his power be manifest. What a difference from every other religion in the world!

2. The second implication of our theme is the warning Christ utters about the severed branch. They are very startling sentences, only blunted by our familiarity with them. Listen:

As the branch cannot bear fruit of itself, except it abide in the vine; no more can ye, except ye abide in me. . . . For apart from me ye can do nothing. If a man abide not in me, he is cast forth as a branch, and is withered; and men gather them, and cast them into the fire, and they are burned.

What astonishing sentences! "I am the vine, and ye are the branches. While the relationship is vital between us, you are filled with life, but if it ceases you are dead, withered. Apart from me you can do nothing." We don't believe it, of course. We point to our marvelous achievements. Look at our great philosophers and their systems! Look at our economists and their theories! Look at our psychological insight! What about our politicians—and if you don't think much of them, what about our scientists? Do you call that nothing?—*And Jesus says: "Yes, nothing!"*

Yet candor forces us to admit that while there has been much development, there has been little progress; for surely progress means getting farther along the road which brings you where you want to be. To talk as though scientific inventions spelled progress is nonsense. Some of us who went through the London blitz know that in those awful years, death in the night was more likely, more widespread, and more horrible than it was before the Romans landed in Britain. We wonder, when fear covers the whole earth with gross darkness, why some people think that salvation is round the corner and can be achieved by some economic trick, by some juggling of politicians, by some new scientific discovery, or by some psychological treatment.

Truly, the world would be a wonderful place if all that man has thought and discovered and invented could be linked up with the loving purposes of God—but cut off from love they count for nothing. In spite of all his efforts, *apart from God man cannot turn prowess into progress*. Man is confused and bewildered and frightened as never before, and but for the fact that God's hand is still on the plastic clay of our humanity, we might—in the face of this new atomic and horrible discovery—sing another *Nunc Dimittis:* "Lord, lettest now thy servant depart in tears, for mine eyes have seen Hell."

Says Toynbee, the great historian: "Fourteen out of the twenty-one great civilizations which this earth has known, are now only of interest to the antiquary." God's workshop floor is littered with the broken pieces of those instruments which he could no longer use. One wonders whether Europe and America will be usable instruments, or be thrown away as unusable like Egypt and Babylon and the rest.

So many branches of our civilization started as expressions of religion. Love was the flowing sap which bound the branch to the parent stem. Our great hospitals are a case in point. St. Bartholomew's Hospital in London was an offshoot from St. Bartholomew's Church and an extension of the church's work. In early days all the doctors at "Bart's" were monks and all the nurses nuns. The treatment was a translation into skill and remedy of the love of Christ. I am making no cheap sneer at a great hospital. Now the treatment is ten times as effective, but ten times less loving. No one would claim that a modern hospital is a recognizable expression of the love of Christ. Your surgeon may be an atheist. As long as he is well qualified no one cares. It is overlooked that men hunger for the love of God as much as for healing, and often the two are more closely connected than some people think.

Similarly with education. It started in the Church. It was initiated by the Church, and men were taught to read so that they could read the Bible and find their way to Christ. But now if I wanted a child really to understand and get hold of the love of Jesus, it would be more satisfactory to send him to a mission school in the heart of an African forest or an Indian jungle than to the state school in England. In a missionary school he would be taught by a person who is a missionary first and a teacher second, and in whose heart the love of Christ is blazing, whereas here in Christian England he *can* be taught even scripture by an atheist, and as long as a teacher is qualified, he is not questioned about his Christian faith.

Is it an exaggeration to say that all this is symptomatic? Outside the Church show me what parts of our civilization are in vital touch with the Vine, and yet some men were surprised that a thousand years of civilization could in a sense fall into the abyss into which Germany fell and we almost fell. If the mains are cut off, all your electric gadgets become junk, and if the branch is cut off from the vine, it withereth. Write down this one sentence on the back of an envelope and brood upon it: "Outside God there is only death."

3. The third implication of our text is the warning and the comfort it contains for the personal life.

As far as warning goes, it is perhaps enough to say that what is true of community life is true for the individual. Separated from God, man has not life enough to maintain his own ideals. What he calls progress he should call development. Progress involves getting nearer to one's ideals and this, apart from God, separated from the Vine, man cannot do. Show me the person who has tried any other way and found it to work. After all the sneers against religion, all the excuses with which we try to silence conscience, after all the experiments, for instance, in "free love," show me the people who in old age, having turned away from God, are content and happy. Remorse shatters their peace. "Nerves" harass their days and eat into the silent night. The goods offered are never delivered. The greatest gift of God, peace of mind, eludes them.

The message of Christ is that though my nature be wilder than the wild vine, and all the fruit of it so far be little grapes that are no more than wild and bitter berries—all stone and skin at that—I can be incorporated into the True Vine, and the life of God can stir within me and transform my life from within. Does anyone know a gardener who has succeeded in making a beautiful rose from a wild brier by influences which only act on the latter from without? Must he not graft a life-giving power which can operate from within? Every gardener understands Christ's words about the Vine.

I believe that quite literally the minds of lovers interpenetrate and feed on one another. I once watched an Indian Christian girl fall in love with a veritable wild youth of the jungle—a frightened, rough, superstitious, wild man from the woods. We teased her about him. But her love and lovely nature penetrated his. Reach after reach of his life was overcome and subdued. It wasn't education that changed him, nor environment, nor passion, but Christian love with all its patience and understanding and courage and faith. Christ offers this love-relationship to us. Abide in me and I in you.

That is our personal hope as it is the hope of the world. It is not within our will to achieve. How long will it take us to learn? How many good resolutions have we made and broken? How often, in some lonely hour, high and holy longings have filled our hearts? When we fell in love, when we married, when for the first time we took our own little child into our arms, how we said, almost savagely within ourselves: "I will be a better man." Or, in some quiet hour in the country, among the silent hills or beside the lonely sea, we made our vows again. Or, perhaps in that sad room when, in the firelight, the shadows of death fell upon some loved form and the dark angel took her beyond our ken, then we made a pact with God. But does it last, doesn't it all prove how true are his words—"Apart from me ye can do nothing—nothing—nothing"?

Jesus will come and abide with you and bring you life. Do the words seem quaint? Let us imagine it is wintertime. In the woods the trees are bare and black. What would be the good of tying leaves of green paper on the barren boughs thrashing in the winter wind? Shall we get pink petals of linen and pin them on the chestnut trees and pretend the spring has come? Yet there is a power within those trees and the spirit of the spring can make them beautiful from within. Speak not to me of reconstruction. The word fills my ears with the sounds of saws and hammers and creaking cranes and noisy engines. "Renaissance"—rebirth, beginning again through the power of another. That is better. That word seems full of the song of birds and the whispering winds and the cleansing rain and the rising sap and the crowning glory of the sunshine.

Jesus says: "I am the vine and you can be branches,

empowered from within with my life flowing into yours."
It is the inner, mystical secret which our fathers preached
for so long. "If any man hear my voice and open the door,
I will come into him." The whole of Christianity is in that
sentence, and everything—yes everything—depends on
whether our response is in the first words of man to God
in the Bible, or the last. The first are these: "I heard thy
voice. I was afraid. I hid myself." The last words of man to
God in the Bible are these: "Even so, come, Lord Jesus!"

III

The Good Shepherd

[Jesus said,] I am the good shepherd.—JOHN 10:11

HOW honorable was the profession of the shepherd among the ancient Jews! But for that fact they could never have so frequently likened God to a shepherd and themselves to his sheep. Eighty times in the Bible God is called "the Shepherd of Israel" and this imagery is employed in some of the most beautiful and tender passages in God's Word. Listen to this: "He shall feed his flock like a shepherd, he shall gather the lambs in his arm, and carry them in his bosom, and shall gently lead those that are with young" (Isa. 40:11). Thus Isaiah, or some unknown prophet during the exile, expresses the nature of God, writing hundreds of years before Christ. And in the last book of the Bible, written about A.D. 100, we find the same imagery employed, though to us the metaphors may seem mixed.

The Lamb which is in the midst of the throne shall be their shepherd, and shall guide them unto fountains of waters of life: and God shall wipe away every tear from their eyes. (Rev. 7:17 R.S.V.)

The best-loved psalm in the world opens with the statement "The Lord is my shepherd," and if we try to substitute for the word "shepherd" almost any of the professions and occupations which men follow, we find that few will fit and we realize how highly regarded the profession of shepherd was. Since the word is used so often of God in the Old Testament, and since Jesus knew, loved, and had pondered over every word of the Scriptures which were so dear to him, one cannot help wondering whether his statement, "I am the good shepherd," did not amount to a divine claim.

I should like to dwell with you for a moment or two on that most valuable and beautiful of all the examples of biblical language about shepherds, namely the Twenty-third Psalm, so that later we may meditate on our text, "I am the good shepherd," with an ability to read more into the word "shepherd" than otherwise is possible.

In my opinion the psalm is a shepherd psalm throughout and is an authentic and reminiscent poem written by David, once a shepherd carrying out his arduous duties among the lonely Syrian hills. He remembers how hard the shepherd must work if the sheep are not to want, and states his faith that God will never let him want, but will even find for him something more than bare needs, namely the rare "green pastures" in which he may relax and "lie down," and the "still waters," which to a sheep, terrified of noisy rushing waters, are so necessary to well-being.

"He restoreth my soul" is a four-word sentence over which we pass so quickly, forgetting that excitement, search, and sometimes tragedy lie behind it. There was an ancient law that if a straying sheep were caught on another's property and could be proved to have been there more than twenty-four hours the owner of that property could claim the sheep. Hence greedy and ruthless owners of land adjacent to grazing lands would dig pits and fix at the bottom of them sharp stakes with the points upward. The pits were then covered with the most succulent turf that could be found, precariously placed over a fragile framework of tree branches. If a sheep strayed on to such a trap, its weight would make it fall into the pit, the stakes would impale it and the depth of the pit smother its cries. Unless the shepherd came quickly, he would lose even the legal right to call it his own. Even the strict laws of the Sabbath were set aside if an animal fell into such a pit, so that the shepherd could reclaim it. "What man shall there be of you," asked Jesus scornfully, "that shall have one sheep, and if this fall into a pit on the sabbath day, will he not lay hold on it, and lift it out?" (See Matt. 12:11; Luke 14:5.) A hostile neighbor who found a strayed sheep on his land would cut its throat and claim the carcass if the latter were cold before the shepherd found it. Many animals find their way home, but not the sheep. The shepherd must seek and find it, leaving the ninety-and-nine, to bring home that lost one *before it becomes the property of another.* "He restoreth my soul" simply means "He brings me back when wandering." This is Christ's great task (see Luke 15:3-7). The Good Shepherd seeks each one lest he become the property of the Evil One. "Simon, Simon," said Jesus to Peter, "Satan hath claimed you back for himself." It is the same idea. Unless the Good Shepherd restored our souls, we should be lost indeed.

"He leadeth me in the paths of righteousness for his name's sake." We are back in days when written recommendations and "references" did not exist. A man who wished to do well as a shepherd must make a name for himself. Once that name was made, a shepherd would not do anything foolish, "for his name's sake." No one would trust his sheep to a shepherd who did not know a true path from a false one. Some apparent paths led along a cliff edge and then just stopped. They were not true paths at all, but just ledges of rock that had broken away and ended in sheer precipice. Sheep on such a path would be in a dangerous situation. Those in front could not go on or easily turn around in their tracks. Those behind would bunch and make any safe extrication almost impossible. Some sheep would be pushed over the edge, and if that happened the shepherd would forever have lost his name as a shepherd. He should never have led his sheep along such a false path.

David feels that God will lead those who trust him along a true path,[1] and though it may be hard and rugged, and pass for a time through the wilderness, the path along which God leads us will do what a true path always does, bring us out where we want to be.

Even the dark valley itself has a path through it which the Good Shepherd has trodden; trodden right through to the sunny uplands beyond, and I want to emphasize in a moment the fact that he will tread it again with us. The original of the psalm does not contain the word "death," and those who have seen the dark and gloomy "wadis" of Palestine can well realize how reluctant a shepherd must have been to take sheep through such dangerous places where thieves and wild animals so often lurk. But any dark ravine can be less trying for the sheep if the shepherd is near. "Though I walk through a gloomy ravine, I will fear no evil for thou art with me."

In his book *My Shepherd Life in Galilee,* Stephen Haboush writes:

I used to dread taking the sheep through one particular valley in Galilee. It is called the Wadi el-naar (the valley of fire). Next to the Dead Sea it is the hottest place in Palestine, being over five hundred feet below sea level. An ancient road runs through this valley; in fact it was the most popular road in the days of Jesus. . . . Though it was the longest way to Jerusalem, the Jews, nevertheless, in the time of our Lord, preferred it to the Samaritan route . . . for the Jews had no dealings with the Samaritans. This valley of fire was a rendezvous of thieves and

---

[1]See Ps. 23:3 (Moffatt's translation).

robbers, also of the wild beasts that harrassed the shepherd and his flock. I would dread leading the sheep through this valley, but it was necessary whenever new pasture ground must be sought on the other side. My sheep would sense the danger and gather closely to my side. My continual calling and the sense of my presence gave them confidence and allayed their fear.[2]

The shepherd normally carried a club, for his was a dangerous profession. Even now there are hyenas and the occasional wolf, and was not David famous for his victory over the lion and the bear? (I Sam. 17:34-35). This club, usually attached to the belt, is called a "rod" in the psalm. The staff was probably the familiar crook; its hooked end was used to pull briers away from a path, or more frequently to pull by its hind leg an errant sheep just beginning to leave the path for the dangerous undergrowth. Resting his arm in the crook end of a "staff" and fixing the other in the ground, the shepherd could rest and even sleep without resorting to a recumbence dangerous in one watching sheep in a perilous place. We remember the verse about Jacob "leaning upon the top of his staff" (Heb. 11:21). A shepherd used his staff to leap over a brook without wetting his feet. And leafy branches of trees could be broken down by the staff for the goats in a flock. What comfort to the sheep to think that the shepherd could deal with every situation that beset them, including the dangers to their well-being!

When the shepherd psalm talks of the prepared table and the overflowing cup, it should not be assumed that its author has deserted the pastoral imagery for a banquet scene. A shepherd who wanted to have his own midday meal could hardly take it if the sheep were scattered in a ravine or glen, or partly out of sight on a

[2]Page 39. Used by permission of Harper & Brothers.

mountain side. He would seek "tables" in the grass; flat meadowland where he could keep the sheep under his eye. But there were certain grasses not very common, yet not infrequent, which the sheep would eat and which were poisonous. Basil Matthews, in his *Life of Jesus Christ*, refers to them, and William Knight, in his book *The Song of Our Syrian Guest*, says that one shepherd lost three hundred sheep by omitting to "prepare the table" beforehand. But other enemies were the vipers and the cobras. In northern Palestine I saw, during a single morning, two deadly cobras in the grass where sheep were feeding. Stephen Haboush says that in Palestine the shepherd goes before his sheep on purpose to deal with their enemies. "Thou preparest a table before me in the presence of mine enemies," noxious weeds and dangerous snakes.

Then comes the anointing of the bruised head as the sheep passes into the sheepfold and the assuaging of its thirst from the big two-handled cup;[3] and the whole flock, shepherded by the dogs that brought up the rear,[4] are safe for the night.

As we meditate on Christ's self-chosen title as "the Good Shepherd," there are four functions of the shepherd I should like to mention which are abundantly true of our Lord and entirely relevant to our lives today.

1. Jesus, the Good Shepherd, is the faithful friend of the sheep. I am told by scholars that in the Old

---

[3]*Op. cit.*, p. 161.

[4]The word "follow" in the sentence, "goodness and mercy shall *follow* me," etc., means, says James Hope Moulton, "follow like a dog." See also Job 30:1, Thomson's *The Land and the Book*, p. 202, and Stephen Haboush, *op. cit.*, p. 49. George Adam Smith translates the original: "Surely goodness and mercy shall *hunt* me." Francis Thompson wrote *The Hound of Heaven* after meditating on the last verse of Ps. 23. Without doubt the author meant us to think of goodness and mercy as the dogs that bring up the rear of an Eastern flock.

Testament the word "shepherd" and the word "friend" come from the same root.

I sometimes wonder if the greatest benefit which the practice of religion confers on those who devoutly try it out is not the sheer fact of a divine friendship. I remember talking to the English philosopher, C. E. M. Joad, about this. He said that the thought which swung him, more than any other, in the direction of religion was that it was intolerable to suppose that a creature like man was left all alone on this planet, without any resources or support save what he could himself manufacture out of his own will power and insight.

That God is *with us* seems to me the golden thread of comfort and sustenance that runs throughout the Bible from beginning to end.

Enoch walked with God. Abraham was called the friend of God. To Moses, also a shepherd, came the message: "I will be with thee." Joshua could be "strong and of a good courage" because the Lord was with him. David, the shepherd, became spiritually a sheep in the care of the Shepherd who never deserted his sheep. It was when Elijah thought he was all alone that his courage broke, but the still small Voice assured him that he was not as lonely as he thought. Elisha felt himself surrounded by the forces of the unseen and the supporting presence of God. So through all the prophets runs the golden thread. Isaiah, Jeremiah, Amos, Hosea, right on to Micah with his simple demand "to do justly, love mercy, and walk humbly *with God*."

Jesus himself, we note, was never the recluse. He was not an oracle living in a cave on a mountain side who had to be consulted by weary pilgrims. He loved to be with them, was criticized for attending parties, and was indeed Immanuel, God with us. How perfectly is the nature of the Good Shepherd revealed in these words: "Seeing the multitude, he was moved with compassion because they were as sheep not having a shepherd." I will give you another Comforter," said Jesus, "that he may be *with you* for ever." "With you"—the words are like a lovely haunting refrain that occurs through all the music of the Bible message. It closes with a picture of the redeemed who are "forever with the Lord." "His servants shall do him service and they shall see his face." What higher reward could they have? What greater bliss can be imagined?

Nowhere are we promised by the Good Shepherd that the journey will be free from wilderness experiences. Nowhere are we promised that all danger will be abolished and all rocks, thorns, and slippery places removed. What the Good Shepherd promises is that he will be with each of his sheep in every experience that befalls. Best of all, what he promises is that they will not lose their way and that at last, without regrets, or remonstrances, or resentment at unjust treatment, they shall arrive where he wants them to be.

2. The second point on which I want our thought to dwell is that the Shepherd goes before the flock.

The Incarnation is unspeakably precious to us in a score of ways, but that God himself should become man is breath-taking in its wonder and appeal.

> Thou knowest, not alone as God all-knowing;
> As Man our mortal weakness Thou hast proved;
> On earth, with purest sympathies o'er-flowing,
> O Saviour, Thou hast wept, and Thou hast loved;
> And love and sorrow still to Thee may come,
> And find in Thee a hiding-place, a rest, a home.

And still the Good Shepherd is "with us." Not only has he passed through this world and worn our flesh, known the limitations, frustrations, and irritations of humble life here, experienced more cunning temptations and keener sorrows than we shall ever know, but is still with us sharing in all that troubles us and pledging himself as the Good Shepherd to bring us safely to the fold at eventide.

In another sense he goes before us. There is a tendency on the part of some to regard him as one who belongs to the past, who lived indubitably a beautiful life, did many beautiful deeds, spoke many beautiful words, and died a noble and terrible death, but then passed, as others have done, into the great silence.

It is important to remember that he not only belongs to the past and the present, but is the King of the future. When we examine the sentence, "I am the Alpha and the Omega," we shall deal with this more fully. Two of Whittier's verses give us part of the truth:

> No fable old, no mythic lore,
>   No dream of bards and seers,
> No dead fact stranded on the shore
>   Of the oblivious years;
>
> But warm, sweet, tender, even yet
>   A present help is He;
> And faith has still its Olivet,
>   And love its Galilee.

But the truth is even more glorious than that. He is in the future. Not left behind on "the shore of the oblivious years," not merely the present help, but the clue to the future.

If he is what Christianity claims, then, so far from being out of date or irrelevant to modern situations, he is supremely relevant. All values are tested by him and, let this be especially remembered, *all progress is toward him*. It is no good our pretending that he can be politely set aside; or our agreeing that no doubt he *was* very wonderful, but is now out of date. Because he is what he

45

THE AUTOBIOGRAPHY OF JESUS

is, all ways of living will be tested by him. We shall find
that all roads lead to disaster which lead away from him.
All heads will be bowed before him at last, however
proudly they are held today, and there awaits everyone
who has not joyfully welcomed it, an inevitable
encounter with him, for he is the personification of what
we vaguely call Reality. No one ever finally bypasses
Reality. In other words, the Good Shepherd will not
forget one of his sheep. Ninety-nine percent is not good
enough for him.

3. The third thought I wish to offer is that Jesus is the
Good Shepherd who keeps the flock together.

A shepherd once told me that when sheep are
troubled, they look up to see if the shepherd is near. If
he is, they are comforted and content. If not, they are
uneasy and almost any disturbance can make them
panic and flee, perhaps breaking away from the main
flock. Knowing that sheep have not very good eye-
sight—they can only see about fifteen yards—when the
shepherd has gathered the sheep to some tableland in
the grass, such as I have described, and wants to recline
on the grass, he will fix his staff upright in the ground
and arrange his coat on it, with his headgear on the top,
so that, glancing up, the sheep think the shepherd is still
with them. Sometimes, however, it happens that the
sheep are not convinced. They suspect the trick. If they
show signs of distress, the *voice* of the shepherd gives
them instant relief.

My sheep hear my *voice*, and I know them, and they follow me:
and I give unto them eternal life; and they shall never perish, and
no one shall snatch them out of my hand. (John 10:27-28)

I am quite sure, in my own mind, that God's final
purpose is to lead all the nations of the world to the

46

realization that they belong to one great family. Each has something to give to the others, and each has something to take. "Other sheep I have, which are not [yet] of this fold: them also I must bring, and *they shall hear my voice;* and they shall become one flock, with one shepherd" (John 10:16).

The unification of the whole world is possible. For world peace it would seem essential. Is there any unification possible save through Christ? I cannot see any hope at all save there. Is this just a pious bit of wishful thinking born of the conventional acceptance of our religion and tainted by our intolerance of other faiths, or do the facts really point that way?

I think the facts point that way. One of the factors that compels me to believe in Christ's divinity is this: He has now been preached to all nations. His words have been translated into all languages. His teaching has reached the hearts of thinkers in every race. Yet there is not one nation that feels he is a foreigner, that his ideal and ideas are out of harmony with its own. Black men, yellow men, red men, brown men, and white men not only revere him, but even claim him as their own.

Imagine for a moment that one were talking to men of another race about any other great human figure. How necessary to paint his background, to note the relationship of his ideas to his period of history, to make due allowance for his training, upbringing, and outlook! But Christ is Everyman to the nth degree of all his possibilities. What he said finds its natural home in every heart. Many of his sayings are very difficult to understand, but this is never because his thought-forms have the limitations of one particular nation or place. What he was is what Everyman knows God meant man to be. We make allowances for ourselves when we do not understand another. "He's Irish," we say. "He's a Catholic, or Socialist, or Jew." Jesus was a Jew, and yet

THE AUTOBIOGRAPHY OF JESUS

that is almost the last thing about him that occurs to us. He belongs to Everyman, is understood by Everyman, is Everyman! Mohammed has made no conquests in the far North, the far South, the far East, or the far West. Hinduism spreads hardly at all. Confucianism makes little appeal to the West, and Eskimos and Hottentots make little of the Buddha. Christ has disciples who would die for him in every country under heaven, including Russia and her satellites. Is there, in fact, any name under heaven through which men can be gathered into a unity save his? "Other sheep I have, which are not of this fold: them also I must bring, and they shall hear my voice; and they shall become one flock, with one shepherd." "When sheep are troubled," said one who had spent his whole life among sheep, "they look for the shepherd." Please God they won't be troubled much longer before they begin to look for the only Good Shepherd who appeals to *all* the sheep!

4. My last point is implied in what I have said already. The Good Shepherd makes us feel that we belong to him.

Said Martin Luther: "The heart of religion is in its personal pronouns." Said the revered and beloved Canon Peter Green of Manchester: "There is no emotion so necessary to a true religion, nor any so fundamental to it, as the sense of belonging to God." What a profound truth those quotations enshrine! I once attended, in the Royal Albert Hall, London, a magnificent rendering of Handel's *Messiah* by a choir of several hundreds. The friend who accompanied me was a dear saint of God, my own father-in-law, then in his seventies. We rose, of course, for the Hallelujah Chorus, and when that inspired song rose to its stupendous heights,

THE GOOD SHEPHERD

King of kings, Lord of lords,
He shall reign for ever and ever, for ever and ever,
  Hallelujah, Hallelujah, HALLELUJAH!

my friend could hardly contain himself. As we resumed our seats, the tears were streaming from his clear blue eyes and coursing down his lined cheeks. When he recovered he whispered to me: "That was *my* Saviour they were singing about!" I have never forgotten, I shall never forget, the meaning he put into that word "my."

Jesus, the Good Shepherd, is willing to say "*my* sheep" about you. Are you willing to say "*my* Shepherd" about him?

IV

The Truth

Jesus said . . . I am . . . the truth.—JOHN 14:6 (R.S.V.)

OUR text in this chapter is a very difficult sentence because we do not commonly identify the truth with a person. We say that a person is truthful, or that he is sincere—the Greek word for truth could be translated, "reality" or "sincerity"—and we think of truth as something which is to some extent attained or discovered by a person. We do not think of truth as identified with him. If we did, it would mean that there was a perfect and inclusive relationship between that person's mind and the whole of reality. Seriously to say "I am the truth" is an awe-ful thing to say in the true sense of that word. For men, from the beginning of time, ever since they began to think at all, have been seeking humbly, reverently, painfully, and persistently for the truth. It has been for them something they sought to reach and they have been the servants of truth. Sir Isaac Newton said:

To myself, I seem to have been only like a boy playing on the seashore and diverting myself in now and then finding a smoother pebble or a prettier shell than ordinary, whilst the great ocean of truth lay all undiscovered before me.

Think of Socrates, Aristotle, Plato, and indeed all the philosophers of all races through all centuries, who would never have claimed to have received more than a fraction of that sublime and ultimate reality, the truth. Yet here is one, who if he is correctly reported, claims to actualize in his person that which all men have been seeking, but which no man has ever found. It is, of course, a claim to divinity. No man has ever said such a thing before. Certainly no sane man will ever again seriously say: "I am the truth." "The ultimate truth," said Archbishop Temple, "is not a system of propositions grasped by a perfect intelligence, but is a Personal Being apprehended by love."[1]

So—and this is true of many other sayings of Jesus—we are driven to the dilemma that this Man is made or else divine in a sense far different from any before him or after him. I am aware, of course, that in the Fourth Gospel we are not to look for the actual words of Jesus. We are rather to regard this Gospel as the profound meditation of one who had been close to him and had pondered his message. At the same time, no one would have dared to make up such a sentence, and it is a sentence in harmony with so many other things he said. How can a mere man say, "I am the light of the world," or "I am the bread of life"? As Charles Gore said, "If this is not superhuman authority that speaks to us here, it is surely superhuman arrogance."

So we are driven to say that here is madness or divinity. It is a strange madness! For if the life that lay behind these sayings is that of a lunatic, it is a lunacy better than our sanity. So we ascribe to Jesus divinity, not knowing all that the word connotes, but meaning, at any rate, that for this Man the word "humanity" alone is too small. Here is God expressed in a human life. Here is Jesus claiming equality with God, about whom alone the words can be true: "I am the Truth."

But I do not want to pursue with you that line of thought. If we did, we should be landed in philosophical and theological speculations which have small relation to

[1] *Readings in St. John's Gospel.*

our day-to-day life. I want rather ask you to look with me at three implications of this profound sentence: "I am the Truth."

1. *It implies that he who seeks the truth is seeking God.* Far more people are seeking truth than we sometimes imagine. Indeed, the bewilderment and uncertainty of our time is symptomatic of this quest. Without putting it into words, people are saying: "What does life mean? Where can the mind rest? What can I really be sure about?" We note the large number of religious sects. Surely they represent a quest for truth. We note the organizations not even labeled sects, and yet containing seekers after truth. This popular cult of Spiritualism and other less well-known sects and movements show the restless minds of men seeking some truth for which they feel hungry, and seizing on some little fragment of truth and, as we think, getting it all out of proportion in their enthusiasm. Let us not brush them aside impatiently. Truth is found in strange places and he who is seeking the truth is seeking God.

Under this heading I would say two things:

a) Let us not forget that truth is often the fruit of insight as well as of purely intellectual quest. Do you remember that lovely passage in the life of Winifred Holtby? A physician had told her she had only two years to live. She was only thirty-three years of age. It was early springtime and she went out for a walk over a hillside and stood by a trough of water which was frozen. Some young lambs were evidently trying to drink. Dejected, bitter, frustrated, rebelling bitterly against her sentence, she broke the ice for the lambs with her stick, and as she did so she heard a voice saying: "Having nothing, yet possessing all things." It was so distinct that she looked round, startled, but she was alone with the lambs on an empty hillside. Suddenly, Vera Brittain tells us, in a flash, the grief, the bitterness, the sense of frustration disappeared.

She walked down the hill with a feeling of exhilaration. Her whole outlook had altered. She felt that in that moment of insight, which afterwards she called her conversion, there came to her such a sense of the truth about God and the world, such an insight into abiding reality, that she felt she could bear anything. That is a way of apprehending truth of which I feel sure our Lord would approve.

Let us notice a very interesting thing. Jesus rarely argued. Very rarely did he ask men to approach truth through the course of an argument. But very often he used the word "Look!" and the word "See!" Sometime when you have leisure, note the times he talked about *seeing* the kingdom of heaven. "Blessed are the pure in heart"—blessed are those whose eyes are cleansed so that they can *see* God. One is reminded of two wonderful lines in Browning's *The Ring and the Book:*

> So may the truth be flashed out by one blow.
> And Guido see, one instant, and be saved.

So, if you are questing for truth, looking for something about which you can be certain, do not imagine, for a moment, that you have to be clever, educated, learned, or well trained in scientific investigation. Blessed are the pure in heart, for they shall have insight into reality. They shall know the truth.

In so many situations Browning's words in "Paracelsus" are true:

> Truth is within ourselves; it takes no rise
> From outward things, whate'er you may believe.
> There is an inmost centre in us all,
> Where truth abides in fullness; and around,
> Wall upon wall, the gross flesh hems it in,
> This perfect, clear perception—which is truth,
> A baffling and perverting carnal mesh

Binds it, and makes all error: and to KNOW
Rather consists in opening out a way
Whence the imprisoned splendour may escape,
Than in effecting entry for a light
Supposed to be without.

When that "imprisoned splendour" does escape we
know without the aid of argument, just as we know that
some music is utterly beautiful, even if we are ignorant
of the laws of harmony and counterpoint. We *know* as
men watching through a long, dark night *know* that the
dawn has come. The Christ within, who is the Truth,
arises and needs no more assistance from the para-
phernalia of intellectual argument than the dawn
needs.

b) But having said that, under this same heading that
seeking truth is seeking God, I do want to say a word
about all we ought to learn as Christian people from the
methods of the scientist. The scientist follows the high,
white star of truth *wherever* it leads him. He is prepared to
give up the most dearly loved preconceived opinion if the
discovery of the truth shows it to be false. He does not
think more of tradition than of truth. He does not
attempt to maintain a uniformity in science by using the
same words century after century, and then making a
mental reservation that those words shall henceforth
carry a different meaning. "Where would the science of
mathematics be," said Oliver Wendell Holmes, "if two
meant two to you, twelve to me, and twenty-two to
somebody else?" The apparent unity of the beliefs of
Christians is spurious if a species of mental dishonesty is
essential to its maintenance. It is one of the dangerous
things about religion that ancient words are repeated,
bluffing the man in the street that they mean what they
say, but concerning which mental reservations and
private interpretations are used to make them mean half

a dozen things. Speaking of the churches, the late Clutton Brock said:

> Their apologetics, when most liberal and intelligent, remain apologetics, having for their aim not the discovery of truth, but the proof that there is still some vestige of truth in Christianity.

It is a stern word, sterner perhaps than we deserve, but I am quite sure that the Church does give the impression of being far keener that orthodoxy and tradition should be maintained, than that the unfolding need of truth should be followed wherever it leads. Many are more concerned to prove that their brand of orthodoxy is the authentic one than to seek the truth and follow it.

I feel certain that this attitude would not have the sanction of Jesus, for Jesus said that the first commandment of all is this: "Thou shalt love the Lord thy God with all thy mind." It is not loving God with your mind to cling to ancient forms when the life has gone out of them, to use words which conceal, more than they reveal, the truth. And part of the trouble of our generation is that religion has lost to science the leadership of the world which once it possessed, because science has always shown herself devoted to the truth and ready to part with musty forms and ancient tradition, however venerable and however often repeated, if the truth leads in a new direction. The loyalty, devotion, and enthusiasm which young people give to science should make religious leaders think.

I sometimes feel ashamed that our young students at school and college, who from Monday to Friday live in an atmosphere in which truth is only accepted if it can be proved, are asked on Sunday to come to church and believe something because it is the traditional teaching of the church. We ask them to believe by faith—and I know how necessary faith is—but we put our case as though to say, "You must believe for there is no evidence," forgetting that "must" and "believe" never go together. To wed them is to make subsequent divorce inevitable when the mind awakens to what has been done to it. Or we ask young people to accept bad reasons and feeble arguments because they are being used on God's side. Anyone would think that we were afraid of Christianity failing unless its traditional doctrines were accepted, as they have been accepted for centuries by some, without any re-examination, but if anything is not true it ought to perish, and the sooner the better.

This all has the most practical application. Part of the distress in which people live is due to the fact that they are trying by repetition to assert the truth of something that is false. They have grown up with certain ideas and never examined them. Many people, if they did examine them, would not dare to discard them. Pathetically enough, many lovers of the Bible are like hard-pressed soldiers, trying to hold a line of defense from Genesis to Revelation. They feel that the line is a bit weak and wobbly where, for instance, Jonah is concerned, or where some of the Old Testament miracles and some of the imprecatory psalms are concerned, but they feel that religious loyalty means that they must not let anything go. But, in the name of honesty, if a thing is demonstrably not true, let us discard it. If we are in doubt, let us label it for the time being *sub judice*. If it is unimportant—like the Virgin Birth—let us say so. I say "like the Virgin Birth," for how can a doctrine be essential to a religion if the Founder of that religion said nothing about it? Only the truth is worthy of the loyalty of the kind of mind God gave us, and only the truth can make us free.

There was a certain Dr. Butts—he was Henry VIII's physician—who drew up a syllabus of prescriptions from which he would fain have allowed no medical man to diverge. Similarly, four hundred years ago, Thirty-nine Articles were drawn up and the Church of England decreed that from them no man should diverge. Since 1571 the church has made no changes in them. What would the health of this country be like if medical men had never followed the moving star of truth? Suppose we were committed to the prescriptions made out in Henry VIII's days! Yet, though the parallel is not a close one and there are many moving minds within every branch of the Church, the quest for truth is hampered for many by the shackles forged hundreds of years ago, and the poor spiritual health of the nation in part reflects that refusal to follow the developing revelation of God.

I am quite sure that hundreds of our fellows need what Christianity could give them and are hungry for it. But they are like shoppers for bread who arrive when the shop has been shut. They see the bread and want it, but they are kept from entering. So men need the truth of our religion, but they are shut out by words which keep them from getting at the truth and feeding on it. They can see the food. They know that Christianity could not have lasted so long if it did not possess the truth. But men are hampered and hindered. The shop is shut by out-of-date barriers and fastened tight with ancient forms and ambiguous words and unnecessary restrictions. To change the figure to that of Milton's famous line—once more

The hungry sheep look up and are not fed.

2. *Second—and this follows from my first point—the search for truth is an adventure which we certainly ought to undertake.* Not for scientific reasons, important as these are. The scientist follows truth for truth's sake, and that is magnificent. But perhaps it is even grander to quest for religious truth because it is realized that only on the truth can man build up his philosophy of life, and that is something every one must possess. The possession of

truth for man cannot, of course, be absolute. For man, truth is often merely the greatest degree of probability in complete loyalty to the evidence. Nevertheless do let us move as the reliable evidence moves. I was interested to find a quotation recently from Harvey's historic book on *The Circulation of the Blood*. Listen! "It is never discreditable to desert error, even though error be sanctioned by the highest antiquity." What a splendid word for us today, coming down the ages from that famous book published in 1628!

I was reminded of that passage in Browning's *Death in the Desert*:

> God's gift was that man should conceive of truth
> And yearn to gain it, catching at mistake,
> As midway help till he reach fact indeed.

Yes, we shall often catch at a mistake, but let our policy be one of always moving on. Let us never hide in demonstrable error. I hope it does not hurt your feelings if I press that point a little and say to you that we must now discount some passages in the Old Testament. Though they are in the Holy Book, we must in all sincerity admit that the book records what men thought about God centuries ago. They, too, were questing for truth, and with less light than we have. So far from disparaging them, they would surely desire—if they could speak to us—that we should quest for truth, using, as they did, whatever light is available, and never hiding in a demonstrable lie. The Ninety-first Psalm says, "A thousand shall fall at thy side and ten thousand at thy right hand, but it shall not come nigh thee," with the promise of angelic intervention against disaster. What chaplain to the armed forces could read that psalm to men on the eve of an attack? Who could say to those brave airmen who defended our liberties in the Battle of

Britain, "A thousand shall fall at thy side . . . but it shall not come nigh thee"? What an insurance religion would become, and how eager would everyone be to pay the premium of piety! Frankly, unless the words are spiritualized out of their original meaning—which is a species of intellectual dishonesty—they are simply not true. Demonstrably they are not true. Jesus said: "Men shall persecute you and hunt you from city to city, and kill you, and think that by so doing they do God service. But fear not them that kill the body and after that have no more that they can do" (see Matt. 10:16; John 16:2; Matt. 10:28). How many of our own people believed that if they said their prayers during the blitz, they would escape destruction, mutilation, and death? What did they feel when the blitz broke their homes, killed their dear ones, ruined their businesses? Their desolation must have been dreadful, but they brought it on themselves for they tried to hide their souls in something that was not true.

Some of us, I am afraid, have poured scorn on men of Eastern lands who say their prayers to an image made in copper, brass, or wood. But let us never forget what Archbishop Temple once pointed out, that a false mental image is just as dangerous as a false metal image, and the danger in idolatry is not the superficial one which makes us scorn the Eastern idolater and say: "How can a metal thing be of use to him?" Indeed your educated Easterner does not worship the image, but the entity of which the image is the symbol. No! The great danger of idolatry and its great condemnation is that an image imprisons an idea and prevents its growing. The idea is frozen, or, to use a better word, petrified in that image of stone, and he who would follow the ever-moving star of truth cannot do so. Too often the image, whether of wood or words, stops the development of the idea.

Jesus said: "I will give you the spirit of truth, and he shall guide you into all truth." *You cannot be guided anywhere if you refuse to move.* Do not scorn the uneducated heathen because of his metal image. Ask yourself whether a creed or hymn has not too often been a mental image, causing you either to stop thinking or to use words and mean either nothing at all or else something which the words certainly do not say, a species of mental juggling which the man in the street calls downright hypocrisy. "You say the words," he says, "but you do not mean them. You mean something else." I can understand his scorn. It is as though a chemist learned in boyhood Dalton's Atomic Hypothesis that an atom is the smallest conceivable part of an element, and that when the discovery of electrons burst on the chemist's horizon, he refused to stop chanting Dalton's Atomic Theory once a week, but inwardly said to himself: "Of course, by 'atom' I mean 'electron.' " No one, for example, who chants the words, "I believe in the resurrection of the body," means what their first author meant. Everyone knows that the atoms of his body have entered other forms of life and become parts of other bodies, some of them human. What are some of our silly sentimental hymns but stupid mental images beyond which we ought to have progressed hundreds of years ago? We still say the puerile words, and anesthetize our mental apparatus by singing them to tunes that "go," but by doing so we refuse the challenge of God: "Thou shalt love the Lord thy God with all thy mind." "Let us sleep," men say. "Don't make us think. We only want to be left alone playing with the mental toys we've loved since childhood."

3. *My third point is that to say that Jesus is the Truth challenges us to sincerity at all costs.* The word "truth" and the word "sincerity" are the same in Greek *(aletheia)*. He only loves the truth who sincerely seeks it. I like that word "sincere" and I expect you know its origin. When marble pillars were made, there might be a flaw in one of them. If

so, the unscrupulous dealer would fill it up with wax *(cera)*. The wax would be polished and it would look exactly like the marble of the rest of the pillar and the pillar would be sold. But when the bad weather came, the flaw would be revealed. Gradually the rain would wash out the wax. The pillar was not *"sine cera."* It was not without wax. When you say, "I am, yours sincerely," you are saying, "I am without wax!" You claim that you are sincere, that you do not pretend to be one thing while all the time you are another.

This is not as easy as it sounds. Most of us live behind a façade. How hard it is to be real people! How hard not to maintain a pretense because we want people to think differently about us than the truth warrants. Let us in the name of the God of truth be "without wax." Let us be sincere whether it is in the matter of being in love, or meeting strangers, or believing the Gospels, or looking into our own heart. Are we really quite convinced that the face that looks out at us from our mirror reveals our true selves, or is that charming, smiling face a mask? "The Word became flesh," says the Fourth Gospel, "and dwelt among us, full of grace and truth," or, if you like it better, "full of winsomeness and sincerity."

Let us approach other people ready to think the best of them and to give them the benefit of any doubt, and let us be slow to tie labels on them. But with ourselves and our own motives let us be starkly ruthless, utterly honest, completely sincere, not forgetting that great dictum of all psychologists that the first law of mental health and inward peace is to be honest about oneself. Said a woman to a psychologist I know in London: "Doctor, do you realize that the happiest day of my life was the day when—after a number of talks with you—I stopped trying to look twenty years younger than I am?" It is a trivial illustration, but underneath it is a principle of the very first importance. We should pray that God would help us to love only the truth, and save us from ever trying to hide in lies, whether about him or about ourselves.

When we move nearer the truth, whether it be the truth about God, or about man, or about the world, or about ourselves, we move nearer to God. "Truth is in Jesus," said Paul.[2] When we move nearer the truth, we move nearer to Jesus, who is himself both the Truth and the Source of our urge to discover it. There can be no aim higher than to move nearer to Jesus. To attempt it is to make progress—the only true progress there is. For he is the Reality behind all men's dreaming, the Clue for which we are all groping, the Answer to all our prayers.

[2]Ephesians 4:21 has been called by Prof. Clive Thexton, "the most misquoted verse in the Bible." People speak of "the truth as it is in Jesus" as if there were another kind which is not in Jesus. "Paul's argument is, 'You did not learn Christ as a Guide unto wantonness: I presume that you were indeed taught in His school, for truth is embodied in Jesus and in Him alone. Then behave like a follower of His.' "

V

Meek and Lowly of Heart

[Jesus said,] I am meek and lowly in heart.—MATT. 11:29

THESE words are set in the midst of one of the greatest and best-loved passages of the New Testament, like a pearl among diamonds. I often think the whole passage must be among the best-loved quotations in the world.

Come unto me, all ye that labour and are heavy laden, and I will give you rest. Take my yoke upon you, and learn of me; for I am meek and lowly in heart: and ye shall find rest unto your souls. For my yoke is easy, and my burden is light. (Matt. 11:28-30)

Let us begin with two questions which reverence may have kept us from asking.

1. Do we really admire meekness? Do we want to be like Jesus if it means being meek? Isn't "meek" a word and a quality repulsive in the extreme? The character of Uriah Heep rushes to the mind—one of Dickens' most revolting characters. A meek man sounds like one without manliness or virility, one who is sycophantic and without what we call a mind of his own.

The truth is that the English word "meek" has deteriorated in character. In our English versions Moses is called "meek" (Num. 12:3). No one would say that that great leader, who dominated the thought and the fortunes of Israel, was without manliness or virility. Perhaps there is little difference in meaning between "meek" and "lowly in heart." Both mean the opposite of "self-assertive," "dominating," "hectoring," "bullying," "self-opinionated."

One of the most obvious marks of real greatness is

lowly-mindedness. I have not met many really great people, but those I have met have always impressed me by that quality. It is the little man who *tries* so hard to impress you with his cleverness or his wealth, his scholarship or importance. Clearly he *needs* to do so. His repressed inferiority, his hidden feebleness creates a great fear that he may be found out to be the ordinary person he really is. The great have no such fear. They know themselves and, because they *are* great, they know how little they know, how unimportant the greatest sons of men really are. They have nothing to cover and they are not always living in a world of silly pretense which they have persuaded themselves is the real world, and so they walk humbly with their fellows. They are meek and lowly in heart and their minds are at rest.

When Albert Schweitzer, certainly one of the greatest living men, stayed in my home years ago, my wife and I were delighted with our guest. To see him sit at our cheap piano with our daughter, then a little girl, on his knee, and to hear and watch him take her little fingers and push them on to the keys as together they hammered out some simple melody, and then to remember that our guest is probably the greatest living exponent of Bach's music, a great philosopher, a great theologian, and a world-famous missionary-doctor, was to be able to imagine what it must have been like to have been with Jesus. There was no conceit, no pride, no assumption of superiority—just a happy man who was perfectly and completely himself and as natural and unaffected with us as he was with our little girl, listening to our ideas as if they had value, seeking our views when they could not possibly have contributed to his wisdom, and doing all this not as one who was condescending, or playing out an act, or setting himself to be patient with us, but as one who was clearly enjoying ordinary human fellowship. My wife and I knew that we were witnessing the true humility of the truly great. How it contrasts with the loud-voiced, truculent egotism of some of the conceited little men with whom one has to deal, men who ride roughly over the ideas and the feelings of others, who think only of themselves, ruthlessly assert themselves in every situation, think no one can do a thing as well as they can do it, seek to extract admiration for themselves from every successful event, and who worship their own egos. They give point to that perfect definition of egotism as "the anodyne which God allows a man to administer to himself in order to deaden the pain of being a fool."

Yes, Jesus was meek and lowly in heart. He washed his disciples' feet. He fled from the adoring multitude. He asked his patients not to ascribe their cure to him, but to "tell no man." Though he was rich, for our sakes he became poor. Though he was the Son of God and could have commanded legions of angels, could always have got his own way, could have scattered his enemies and commanded worship from his followers, yet he humbled himself to the lowest level, and, counting it not a prize to be on an equality with God, he took the form of a slave. He became obedient unto death, even the death of the cross. He was meek and lowly in heart.

But a second question obtrudes, though reverence makes us slow to ask it. Why should he say so? Would Schweitzer say "I am meek and lowly of heart"? Let others say it about the great, but does a great one assert it of himself? When a man asserts his virtues, we normally think that the assertion detracts from the virtue.

I have meditated long on this and feel that the answer is in the context of the whole passage. Jesus had been using the most violent language. We read that

he began to upbraid the cities wherein most of his mighty works were done. . . . Woe unto thee, Chorazin! woe unto thee,

Bethsaida! for if the mighty works had been done in Tyre and Sidon which were done in you, they would have repented long ago in sackcloth and ashes. . . . And thou, Capernaum, shalt thou be exalted unto heaven? thou shalt go down unto Hades. . . . It shall be more tolerable for the land of Sodom in the day of judgement, than for thee. (Matt. 11:20-24)

Matthew takes pains to tell us that it was "at that season" that Jesus so rapidly changed his tone and spoke the tender words of invitation which we have been considering. One feels that the evangelist wants us to realize that the upbraiding and the invitation to the heavy laden were spoken as he reports them, namely on the same occasion and in close proximity. I have wondered whether Jesus saw that his vehemence frightened them and had to say, "I am meek and lowly in heart," to prevent a misunderstanding which might have driven them from him. So we might say to children who had witnessed some outburst of "righteous indignation" on our part: "Come here, I won't bite you. I'm a mild man really." It would not be boasting in such a situation, just as it would not be boasting for a businessman who felt he was being treated with some misgiving, or even suspicion, to say: "I'm an honest man. I won't defraud you."

Jesus, one feels, must often have taken pains so as not to leave a false impression on people's minds. It is surprising that for some people today he wears the label "Gentle Jesus, meek and mild." "Ye serpents, ye offspring of vipers, how shall ye escape the judgement of hell?" (Matt. 23:33). That doesn't sound particularly gentle, or meek, or mild. Most of his language to the hypocrites is not gentle. He has blasted the name of the Pharisees forever, though no doubt some were quiet and kindly old gentlemen, with carpet slippers and inoffensive manners. He said that one who offended one of his little ones would be better thrown into the sea with a heavy stone tied round his neck (Matt. 18:6). Nothing gentle about that!

He said about Judas that in the light of what was coming to him, "better were it for that man that he had never been born" (Matt. 26:24). When flattering women thanked him for his sermon, he snubbed them with: "Yea, rather, blessed are they that hear the word of God, and keep it" (Luke 11:28). He said he had come to bring "not peace, but a sword," and to separate the members of a family from one another (Matt. 10:34). His purposes and prophecies involved the coming of the day when the women who had never had babies would be considered the lucky ones (Luke 23:29). He called his dearest and most faithful friend "Satan" (Matt. 16:23), and when Peter pledged his loyalty, Jesus bluntly told him that before the dawn he would have gone back on his word (Matt. 26:34).

We know *now* that his heart was filled with a passionate love, that the measure of his violence with the Pharisees was the measure of the thickness of their armor against the shafts of truth. We know that he warned men that love is austere as well as gentle, and of the nature of steel as well as flowers; that conscious disobedience brings untold misery, and that while forgiveness restores relationship, it does not remit penalty. Sin was what he came to smash. What else could he do but hit it as hard as he could? Jesus never pandered to the sloppy views of today by which we deceive ourselves that "we are all going the same way," and that "all will be the same in the end," as though God were a kind of indulgent grandpa who will meet us at death and pat us all on the head, say to us concerning our sins, "Well, well, I'm sure you didn't mean it," give us a bedtime cookie and send us all up to heaven.

He who had the gentlest lips in the world said the most terrible words about sin ever spoken in history. He who had the kindest heart in the world is responsible for the doctrine of hell which no complacent treatment of the Gospels can excise, whether it be a complacency born of scholastic knowledge or of wishful thinking. Granted that our grandfathers caricatured his words and added fantastic horrors of their own to his warnings, but what a counter-caricature it would be wishfully to imagine a "gentle Jesus" and forget that it was he who used expressions like "lost" (Luke 15:24-32), "dead" (*ibid.*), "the age-long fire" (Matt. 25:41), "the shut door" (Matt. 25:10), and "the outer darkness" (Matt. 25:30).

Perhaps then, lest men fled in terror from his violence, he called them to come: "Come unto me." Lest their guilt should drive them from him, he showed his compassion for "the weary and the heavy laden." Perhaps to counteract what must have seemed like his restlessness—for he was ever moving about and urging his disciples on—he told them of the inner rest he could offer. Perhaps, lest men should hear only his upbraidings and form a false conclusion which would make them think he was too exalted for lowly folk like themselves, he told them that he himself bore a yoke and was meek and lowly of heart.

Jesus says that *because* he is meek we are to take his yoke. "Take my yoke upon you, and learn of me; *for* I am meek and lowly in heart." This sharing of the yoke must be looked at carefully. The word "yoke" is derived from the same root as the word "yoga" and we need something of this Eastern discipline in our Western world. Let us look at some pictures that will help us to feel our way into Christ's meaning.

Look at Jesus in the carpenter's shop. He endured it for twenty years. That is a long time, longer than a "life sentence" in English law. In his breast a fire was burning which grew brighter and hotter each day. He growingly *knew* that he stood in a unique relationship *with* God and had a divine mission to accomplish *for* God. How eager he must have been to give all his time and strength to such a task! But he had to wait God's time. "I do only the things that please Him," he said later (John 8:29). So he melted glue, swept up shavings, and searched for nails. He made doors that would open easily and—it is said—made, at Rome's command, crosses for criminals. He made yokes too.

> The yokes He made were true,
> Because the man who dreamed
> Was too
> An artisan.
> The burdens that the oxen drew
> Were light.
> At night
> He lay upon His bed and knew
> No beast of His stood chafing in a stall
> Made restless by a needless gall.[1]

On some days his contribution to the kingdom of God was contentedly to make a yoke so smooth and easy, so well fitted to the bovine shoulders for which it was made, that it would not chafe or irritate. His yokes were always "easy." Years afterwards he said to his weary and fretted listeners: "Come unto me. . . . Take my yoke. . . . My yoke is easy." But he qualified himself to say such a thing because, for a score of years, he trained himself, under the guiding hand of God, to accept the discipline of the ordinary, knowing that God would use it when the time came. He was not too proud or too "set up with himself" to work at humdrum tasks. God would not allow one day of his training to be meaningless if he were obedient day by day to the vision and the voice within. He was meek and lowly in heart. So, with a breath-taking humility, the Lord of Glory earned his authority and his reward, for before he had preached one sermon or worked one miracle, the

[1] From "My Yoke Is Easy" by Gladys Latchaw.

Voice he trusted and loved and followed, said: "This is my beloved Son, in whom I am well pleased" (Matt. 3:17).

Turn now to another picture, that of the Eastern way of plowing. With a projector and a screen I could show you from my own slides what is called a "training yoke." The Mosaic law forbade an ox and an ass being yoked together with an ordinary yoke because, to use a modern idiom, the ass "couldn't take it." When a young ox was being trained for plowing, a training yoke was devised. The younger animal was yoked to the older, stronger, and more experienced animal. The heavy end of the yoke was the burden of the stronger. The stronger was placed at the end of the furrow. The stronger kept straight in the furrow, under the guidance of the plowman. All the weaker had to do was to keep steadily "pulling his weight," as we say, and keeping parallel to the stronger. If, in youthful, bovine pride, the smaller animal pulled away to some fancied path of his own, of course trouble followed. The furrow would have to be plowed again unless the younger accepted the discipline of both the yoke and the goad. Any such action would make the yoke chafe the shoulders of *both animals* and could rub them red-raw. The younger animal during his training must drop his pride, be meek and lowly in heart, give up his will to the stronger, who took the responsibility as well as the burden. Then, for the younger, the yoke would be easy and the burden light.

Isn't all this very relevant for those of us who want to follow Christ? He is not the Arch-Dictator. Even he, the Son of God, was meek and lowly of heart. He put himself under discipline. In the carpenter's shop he learned to accept the yoke of the Father's will for each day, and without chafing against delaying humdrum tasks, believed that God would use every experience in his final plans.

So when God's will opened out for him and he taught his little, weaker brothers, he was concerned with the fret that showed in their faces and the weariness that shadowed their lives. "Come unto me, all ye that labour and are heavy laden, and I will refresh you. If you will be humble and teachable and share with me a training yoke, I will tread the heavy furrow of your life with you. Give your will up to me as I do to my Father. Just pull your weight and keep in step with me. The burden and the responsibility are mine. Realizing this, you will stop fretting and worrying, and you will find inner rest to your souls. My yoke will prove easy for you, and because the burden is mainly on my shoulders, it will be light for you."

Years ago when I was only in my teens, I came across some words which George Eliot quoted from Thomas à Kempis. They so impressed me that I copied them into the blank page at the end of a pocket Methodist hymnbook that our minister at home gave to me. Here they are:

If thou seekest this or that and wouldst be here and there to enjoy thy own will, thou shalt never be quiet nor free from care. For in everything there will be somewhat lacking and in every place there will be some that cross thee. . . . On this sin, that a man inordinately loveth himself, almost all dependeth, but this evil, if it is overcome and subdued, there will presently ensue great peace and tranquility. . . . Forsake thyself . . . then shall all vain imaginations, evil perturbations and superfluous cares fly away. Then shall immoderate fear leave thee and inordinate love shall die.

As I look back on the many failures of my own life, I can see how many of them are due to a refusal of this part of Christ's message. I have not been ready to be meek and lowly of heart. I have wanted my own way and, like a restive young bullock, have refused the yoke of self-discipline and been sure I knew a better way. I have even used God as a means to obtaining my ends as many a preacher is tempted to do. So I have hurt and hindered Christ and rubbed myself red-raw with my demand that I should choose my own path and myself take the responsibility of arriving at some self-chosen goal.

Now, as the eventide of my life begins, I am beginning to understand what should have been clear from the beginning. Of course, the field is his and so is the plowing. The responsibility of the harvest is his also. "For us the trying," said T. S. Eliot, "the rest is not our business." For me only the pulling, keeping in step with him. "In His will," said Dante, "is our peace." It is the only peace in the world. "If," says the blessed à Kempis, "thou wouldst be here and there to enjoy thine own will, thou shalt never be quiet nor free from care."

Rest, of course, is not idleness, but harmony: accepting, not constantly rebelling against, the yoke. Even ambition is not wrong, as the parable of the talents makes clear, as long as ambition is within his will and in *his* furrow instead of our own.

A girl in her early teens made this clearer for me. Her mother was suddenly taken to the hospital, and on her young shoulders came the sudden responsibility of running the home. There was the father's evening meal to prepare and the care of younger children and the household tasks. At last the mother was well enough to take over responsibility. The lassie did pretty well the same things as before, for she had always lent a willing hand in the busy home, but now the direction, the burden of responsibility was her mother's. Oh what a relief for the child! What rest for her mind! She only had to do what she was told as well as she could.

If only we could feel that One, infinitely wise, who knows the end from the beginning, would walk with us, not only sharing our burden, but carrying the heavy end of it himself; if only we could feel that if daily we submitted our wills to his and pulled our best, then he would guide us and accept the responsibility of bringing us to the end of our appointed furrow, whether the world called it success or failure, then we should discover the secret of an inner peace which nothing on earth could destroy. It's worth trying, isn't it? Jesus only makes one condition, that we get our conceited *selves* off our hands and learn of him to be meek and lowly of heart.

VI

The Light of the World

[Jesus said,] I am the light of the world: he that followeth me shall not walk in the darkness, but shall have the light of life.—JOHN 8:12

WE are to think in this chapter of Jesus as the Light of the world. Let us begin by making an imaginative effort to understand just how much that phrase must have meant to the early Christians of the first century.

First of all, we must picture their home-life. When we think of spending a long winter evening, we think of the fireside, the steady light, the books we can read, the music to which we can listen, and perhaps the television program which we can watch. But try to imagine what it must have been for all but the most wealthy people living in the first century. Their homes were only imperfectly weatherproof. The poor had no furniture, no fire, no light, unless perhaps a rush light giving an unsteady glimmer while they partook of their food, no books, no music, little social intercourse or cheery fireside conversation. We can imagine how gloomy, dismal, and uncomfortable the long, dark winter nights must have been, and how passionately men longed for the longer days and shorter nights, for the warmth of the sun and the cheerful return of spring.

But that physical darkness and misery were matched by a spiritual darkness more gloomy still. It was only when I went to India that it dawned on me how full a pagan mind can be of a dark terror that is unknown to most of us. I have met people whose minds were unillumined by the

Christian faith, and who shuddered at the sound of palm trees in the night wind. It was a devil chattering in the darkness. I have met people terrified of the black night, and the shape of the clouds scudding across the moon, and the moan of the sea, and the shriek of the tempest. There was an evil spirit even in a waterfall, a demon in the thunderstorm, and if unfortunately one fell ill, the disease was evidence that one was in the clutch of evil powers.

No one today can have any real understanding of the depth of joy in the heart of the evangelist when he could write down these words: "This is the message which we have heard from him, and announce unto you, that GOD IS LIGHT, AND IN HIM IS NO DARKNESS AT ALL" (I John 1:5). The sky was swept clean of filthy shapes. The light was robbed of obscene horrors. Nature, though still terrifying, was but an expression of the mind of God and meant no evil. The heart of the universe was friendly and the whole world was full of his glory. His ultimate Name was Love and behind all that still seemed mysterious, one lived forever who was the Saviour, Friend, and Lord of all who would receive him. He was, indeed, the Light of the world.

> No flickering torch, no wavering fire,
> But Light, the Life of men.
> Whatever clouds may veil the sky,
> Never is night again.[1]

Never! Just as you cannot halt the sun as it rises on a June morning and push it back again so that night overcomes the glory of the day, so no one can ever live again as though Jesus Christ had never been born. The Sun is risen and men have seen the light. They will never be satisfied with the darkness again and no one for long will

---

[1]From "Never Night Again" by Lilian Cox. Used by permission.

be able to impose it upon them. "The dayspring from on high hath visited us to give light to them that sit in darkness and in the shadow of death" (Luke 1:78-79 K.J.V.).

No wonder the early Christians celebrated the birthday of Jesus, not at the time of year when he was actually born, but when the earth swung back again to the light of spring. Jesus was probably born in April. Shepherds do not watch their flocks by night in December. The sheep at that time are safely folded, for often there is snow on the hills of Palestine in the winter. Jesus was probably born on a night in spring, but the early Christians had no holiday then and could not have celebrated the exact day even if it had been known to them. Many of them were slaves— there were a million slaves in Rome alone and sixty million in the Roman Empire at this time—and when on December 25 their Roman masters gave them a holiday either for the Roman Saturnalia; or else in celebration of the birthday of the god Mithras, the "god of the morning," who had made a treaty of friendship with the sun; when the Romans themselves rejoiced that the days were growing longer and lit huge bonfires in the streets, to give strength—as they believed—to the Sun God, who appeared on wintry days to have become so weak and feeble, then the Christians saw their chance and celebrated the birthday of him who was more to them than the coming of spring, Jesus, the Light of the world.[2]

It is very cheering and heartening to look *at* a light and men who saw the face of Jesus were blessed indeed. Paul

[2]Mithras, a god of Persian origin, was added to the Roman pantheon about 68 B.C. By A.D. 200 Mithraism had spread throughout the Roman Empire and no doubt influenced early Christianity. It demanded moral goodness. Mithras was bent on destroying every form of evil and was sometimes called The Lightbringer. Mithraism has many attractive features.

wrote to the Corinthians thus: "We see the light of the knowledge of the glory of God in the face of Jesus Christ" (II Cor. 4:6). It must have been wonderful indeed just to see his face with the light of heaven shining through his eyes and flashing in his words and deeds.

I am reminded of that lovely and true story of Edward Windsor, when, as Prince of Wales, he went to India.[3] Here was the son of the supreme power, to the outcaste people almost divine. As he drew near the Delhi Gate on one of his journeys, twenty-five thousand outcastes awaited his coming. They only expected to see a car flash past and, with luck, to catch a glimpse of him. While the high caste spectators wondered at his lack of princely pride, Edward, Prince of Wales, ordered his car to be stopped. A spokesman of the untouchables ventured forward and offered, in a little speech, the love and loyalty of the sixty millions of the "unclean." They begged the heir to the throne to intercede for them with his father, the King Emperor, that they might never be abandoned and left to the tyranny of those who despised them and would keep them slaves.

The Prince listened patiently and then did an unheard of thing. He stood up—stood up for them "the worse than dogs"—spoke a few words of kindness, looked them all over slowly, gave them his radiant smile and brought his hand up in a salute. Eyewitnesses said that a strange word was used about that deed which had never had precedent in the whole history of that ancient land. "Behold!" they said, "The light! The light! Did you not see the light upon his face?"

What must it have been to see the light of the knowledge of the glory of God in the face of Jesus Christ as, in the name of his Father God, he gave his word to an outcast world never to leave it or forsake it, to proclaim

---

[3] In *Mother India* by Katherine Mayo.

release to the captives, the recovering of sight to the blind, to set at liberty them that are bruised and to proclaim the acceptable year of the Lord!

It is not a good thing to look *at* the light, but a light does not exist to be looked at. It exists to light up other things. It is good at any time to remember the blazing days one sometimes has in summer. Perhaps we can spend some of them out of doors, yet, unless we happen to be out when the sun is setting, we never look at the sun at all. Almost every part of our enjoyment depends on the illumination of the sun. Yet we do not look at the light. We look at what the light reveals. And it is the same in our own homes. We turn on the light to look for a book, or to read it, and perhaps never glance at the light itself.

Here, if I may, I want to interpose a parable. Imagine that I have—as, indeed, I have—a friend who is a jeweler. Let us imagine that I reach his house long after dark. Let us imagine that he has just been promoted and is in charge of a jewelry business of which he is very proud, and that he says to me, "Although it is so late, I do want to show you my shop. It is just round the corner. Come with me and see it." So, although it is dark and late, I go with him and we enter the shop and I wonder why he keeps me waiting in the dark. He is removing the covers from some of the showcases. Then suddenly he turns on the electric light. In the fraction of a second a thousand reflections reach my eyes from the shining silver and the jewels in the cases before me. They have no light of themselves, but as soon as he turns the light on, every one of them leaps up at me with a message: "Though we have no light within ourselves we reflect the light that is above us."

Let us remember that Jesus not only said: "I am the light of the world"; he said: "Ye are the light of the world." And when we begin to think of some of our Christian friends, the people who have made life rich and meaningful to us, we realize that though perhaps they have no spiritual light of themselves, their lives are beautiful because they continually reflect his. They fling back into this dark world a radiance that they get from him. It is part of my message that we can do that too. Can he count on us to reflect him, or have we become too tarnished, too dusty to care? "Let your light *so* shine before men, that they may see your good works and glorify your Father who is in heaven."

I think we ought to realize also how many splendid enterprises in the world take their radiance from him. If I may change the figure from that of light and imagine civilization as a fabric, do let us realize that if we removed from the woven fabric we call civilization every thread that is in it because of what Jesus said or did or was, we should only have a tattered rag left. Civilization would relapse into the barbarities which we thought had gone forever with what we called the Dark Ages, but which we found showing themselves in places like Belsen and Dachau in the incidents of yesterday.

But as I go, in imagination, into the lighted jeweler's shop, I find that the light reveals not only the splendor of the jewels, but also those things that ought not to be there at all. A cobweb, let us imagine, or dusty shelves, or wastepaper carelessly thrown down and littering the shop. While the darkness reigned in the shop, I did not know they were there; but as soon as the light is turned on, they are apparent. In this sense, too, Jesus is the Light of the world. Men walked in darkness and did not always know what the darkness covered. When Jesus blazed into the world, men knew that certain things they had always accepted were wrong. "This is the judgement," says John, "that the light is come" (John 3:19).

How well I remember a man and his wife who returned to their London flat after a holiday. They had left instructions that the servant should have it dusted and ready for them. In the dusk they arrived and the man sank into his armchair saying: "It's good to be home again. The flat looks very attractive." But his wife wasn't satisfied. She switched on the electric light and drew her finger along the top of the piano. "It's dusty," she said. When the light was turned on, the dust was apparent even to the man! "This is the judgement, that the light is come." We hate things in our own lives about which pagans had no conscience at all. It is because Jesus has turned on such a light that dirty immoralities and dusty deeds are now seen to be wrong. It is true socially. Young men in pagan days were trained to war, and although we may not have seen the last of war, men loathe it as never before.

Socially or individually we can find out whether things are right or wrong by simply letting the Light of the world shine upon them. Let him stand beside you, in imagination, as you do this contemplated thing, or take this risky adventure, or cover up your conscience with excuses and lies, and in the light of his presence you will see what is wrong and realize that it ought not to be there.

The third thing that I want to say about the parable of the jeweler's shop is this. When the jeweler turned on the light, even I, without much knowledge of jewelry, could see the difference between paste and diamonds. Paste gives back a white light, but a real diamond gives back blue. In the blaze that streams from the Light of the world, we can distinguish true values from false.

Who has not watched people fighting, struggling, saving, exhausting themselves to get their hands on what they thought would make life rich and happy, only to find that they got something that was paste? It had a meretricious flash about it, but no real value. Some superiority over others, some place of importance, some coveted distinction, some social status, some fancy qualification—men and women set these things before them and say, "If only I could get that," and when they have got it, it does not do what they thought it would do: make them rich with that interior wealth which is the only enriching thing there is.

How easily deceived we are; how intoxicated by false values! So much so that Jesus himself seems to some people a gloomy darkness which they shun, and his cross a shadow that they fear. So men who still clutch at pagan values, cry with Swinburne:

> Thou hast conquered, O pale Galilean;
> The world has grown grey from Thy breath.

Gray? It seems gray to the pagan, as it did in olden days, for the pagan says: "Let's give rein to our instincts. To hell with these conventional rules and this sentimental nonsense about loving our brother. Let the weakest go to the wall. Let the strong man show his strength by dominating others. Who is this Jesus with his anemic gospel of self-sacrifice, who asks us to stay and help the one broken by the wayside and forget our self-interests for a time? Away with him! We must play for our own hand and look after Number One and assert ourselves. His is no path of light to tread. It is the way of darkness."

O Pan, you god of the Greeks, when you played your pipes, you lured so many along the path that seemed the way of happiness as they danced away toward Arcady! O Mars, you god of the Romans, you brought that ancient empire to world domination and men thought you knew the way to self-realization! Bacchus, men have followed you and believed that your drug was an elixir of life. Venus, how many have lost everything for an erotic love that could not last! False gods do not belong only to the distant past. Hitler, you beguiled young men of Christian families, made them forswear their Christian faith, led them back toward paganism and toward a darkness deeper than death. Karl Marx, we read your stinging words, and millions have followed you because they thought you knew the way and were, indeed, the light of the world. But now we turn and look at ancient Greece and Rome. We contemplate modern Germany and Russia, and we know that, like the will o' the wisp, you led men into a morass and the end was darkness.

Look for a moment at his last imaginative picture. Here is a great banqueting hall in ancient Rome, on the tables is every possible thing to eat and drink; round the tables are noblemen and women, wearing wonderful robes and glittering dresses, enjoying themselves to the full. Imagine the scene to be full of pagan splendor, with wonderful music stealing through the room. Imagine that feast going on and on through the night, an orgy of eating and drinking and making merry. Then imagine that through the windows facing the East, there rises the slow, majestic, steady, certain light of dawn, until the guttering candles seem an insult to its glory. As the sun rises higher in the sky, what a dejected, vulgar, dismal scene it is, with men drunk and women disheveled, with candles guttering and people stupid with wine! Yes, when the Dawn comes, all other lights fail and *all false ways of living are betrayed.*

> O glory of the lighted mind.
> How dead I'd been, how dumb, how blind.

Was he wrong, this gentle Galilean, whom we believe to be the Son of God? Was it a false way of living to spend his life for others and to give himself at last for love of all the world? Or is not this poor, broken world becoming a little less sure of itself, a little conscious that it has followed many false lights, that there are not many lights left to follow, that once again, indeed, the lights that seemed so steady and bright may be going out? In imagination, I see the silent, unquenchable, challenging light of Dawn, and hear a Voice that speaks with an assurance no other voice contains. "I am the light of the world: he that followeth me shall not walk in darkness, but shall have the light of life."

VII

The King

Pilate therefore said unto him, Art thou a king then?
Jesus answered, Thou sayest that I am a king. To this end
have I been born, and to this end am I come into the
world.—JOHN 18:37

THERE is a drama and a flashing brilliance about this
conversation which, in the English version, we partly
miss.

Pilate, the representative of Imperial Rome; Pilate, the
Viceroy, the representative of, in his sense, the only king
worthy of the name, looks at this lonely Figure before
him, hands bound together behind his back, his face pale
with sorrow and mental pain, and wonders what to make
of the charge that he is a serious competitor with Caesar.

The whole company . . . rose up, and brought him before
Pilate. And they began to accuse him, saying, We found this man
perverting our nation, and forbidding to give tribute to Caesar,
and saying that he himself is Christ a king. (Luke 23:1-2)

Pilate's question was much more vivid than the text above
suggests. It was vivid, staccato, incredulous, thus: "*You,*
are *you* a king?"

Let us note with wonder our Lord's answer. If he had
said, "Yes!" he would have given one false impression. If
he had said, "No!" he would have given another. If he had
said, "Yes!" Pilate would have thought that Jesus pleaded
guilty to the charge, that he meant that he was a king in
Pilate's sense. If he had said, "No!" he would have denied
a still deeper truth, for in a very real sense which we must

study, he was and is and will forever be a King. So Jesus said: "Thou sayest that I am a king. To this end have I been born, and to this end am I come into the world." In Pilate's sense of the word "king," the answer was "No!" In the deepest sense of the word, the answer was "Yes!"

J. B. Phillips, in his translation of the Gospels, wipes away all ambiguity. In answer to the question he translates Jesus' reply thus: "Indeed, I am," but I rather cling to the nuance explained above, although the fact that Christ was claiming kingship is attested indubitably by the remainder of his answer: "To this end have I been born, and to this end am I come into the world."

As I understand him, Dr. Temple, the late Archbishop of Canterbury, rather supports the idea that Jesus gave a double answer on purpose, a kind of *double entendre*.[1] Some of his actions would seem to support this. At one point men "came by force and sought to make him a king, but he departed thence" (John 6:15), as though to repudiate earthly kingship. Indeed, to have accepted it could only have ended in bloodshed and the defeat of much nobler and more important ends than earthly kingship could attain. Yet no one who did not claim kingship in some sense could say the things that Jesus said. For instance, to Pilate but a few moments earlier he had said, "My kingdom is not of this world, else would my servants fight" (John 18:36), and in yet earlier sayings he refers to "the Son of man coming in his kingdom" (Matt. 16:28). To his disciples he said:

Ye are they which have continued with me in my temptations; and I appoint unto you a kingdom, even as my Father appointed unto me, that ye may eat and drink at my table *in my kingdom*. (Luke 22:28-30)

[1] His *Meditations on the Fourth Gospel, ad loc.*

Those who tell us that Jesus never claimed divinity might well consider the way in which Jesus talks ceaselessly about the kingdom of God and the kingdom of heaven, bids us pray, "Thy kingdom come," and then speaks of "My kingdom," and refuses, on the occasion of his triumphal entry, to rebuke those who cry: "Blessed is the King that cometh in the name of the Lord" (Luke 19:38, 40). Perhaps the point cannot be pressed, but it seems significant to me. Who is this who has the right to give to any man the keys of the kingdom of God and declare who in it is the greatest? (Matt. 16:19; 18:1).

At any rate the early Church delighted in his kingship. The first piece of literature in the world about Jesus, however sarcastically intended, called him a king. It was the superscription at the top of his cross—"Jesus of Nazareth, the King of the Jews" (John 19:19). And very soon, as has been so often the case with him, words used as a taunt became precious to his followers. Both Paul and John call him "King of kings, and Lord of lords." The word "reign" used of him occurs repeatedly in the New Testament, and the word "throne" occurs over thirty times in the book of Revelation alone. Paul places him "far above all rule, and authority, and power, and dominion, and every name that is named, not only in this world, but also in that which is to come" (Eph. 1:21). "He must reign," we are told, "till he hath put all his enemies under his feet" (I Cor. 15:25).

This tremendous drama, in which the early Christians have been allowed to play a part, is seen to have world-wide significance. Here is no local puppet king. Certainly they will accept the gibe that he is the King of the Jews, but they know he is the King of the Gentiles too, and that every living man, woman, and child is his subject and owes allegiance and loyalty to him. The Christian Church believes that in the end all humanity will fall before him and crown him Lord of *all*.

One of the loveliest stories that comes to us out of the reign of Queen Victoria, I think, is the story of the day when Handel's "Hallelujah Chorus" was first given in the Albert Hall, London. There, in the royal box, sat the young queen, and to her came a lady-in-waiting who said to her: "Madam, when the Hallelujah Chorus is sung, the audience will rise, but it is correct etiquette for Your Majesty to remain seated." But when the vast choir reached the words, "King of kings and Lord of lords," then the young queen rose in her box and stood with downcast eyes for the remainder of that tremendous piece of music. She never did a more queenly thing in her life, and throughout the history of the Christian Church his followers have joyously accorded to Christ that title—King!

But now let us note three things which this idea of the King might suggest to our minds: the sneer, the vision, and the challenge.

1. The sneer. Of course, someone may say: "It is all very well to sing hymns like, 'O worship the King' and 'The King of love' and 'Earth rejoice, the Lord is King,' but can this word really be used in any true sense?" I can imagine the cynic would dwell upon some of the evils which curse our civilization, some of the horrors that darken our community life—the poverty, the slums and the squalor, the sexual vice, and the cruelty to children, so terribly common in our midst; the loveless homes, the suffering, and particularly the suffering that goes on unillumined by any sort of light of kindliness and love. For, in brackets, when we have described all that suffering can do in the way of disciplining our nature and being a wonderful example to others, it is only right to realize that the suffering of a great many people is a dreadful thing, unillumined by that kind of spirit. I have gone into homes where the sickbed of some loved

one is really a center of spiritual power, where from that frail form on the bed there is emitted all the time a bright and spiritual light. But it would be silly and very far from the facts to suppose that that is always, or even generally, true. I could take you to a home where a young girl suffers whose body was operated on by a surgeon, who, it is alleged, blundered. If you go into that room, you are not met with any sort of friendly reception, nor anywhere in that home is there one person who thinks that, after all, God is love and that everything will one day be explained and woven into God's plan. You are met with threats and curses which come from the bed. The patient's face is so distorted with anger, pain, and resentment that it seems as if the personality behind it were invaded by some malignant fiend. The poor girl, though sane, tears at her own nightdress, bites her hands in her agony, and curses God and all who look after her. Or I could take you to a wealthy home where a man lies ill, of whom his own son said to me only recently: "His attitude to his sufferings, his horrible spirit, and the cruel and blasphemous things he says to us have poisoned our home from the day he fell ill." So, in quite wealthy homes, and, at the other end of the scale, among the very poor, there are situations which appear to deny flatly the reign of a King of Love. If you are in the mood, and let your imagination rest on this evil and on that, on this thing that is rotten and on that, on this problem and on that, you might very easily join in the cynic's chorus that says: "It is one thing to sing on a Sunday morning, 'O worship the King,' but where is the King and in what sense does he reign? What power has he got? Behold how many things flaunt his regal authority!"

2. So I think we should pass on to the vision of the King, and show that when all these things that seem to deny his reign have been admitted, we can still claim that Jesus is King.

We have on the throne Queen Elizabeth II, young, charming, untried, if you like, but well trained by her parents, courageous and dedicated. Surely no king or queen in history has expressed the vows to her people which Elizabeth expressed when she came of age. I am going to give myself the pleasure of listing them for you, for they should be known all over the world.

I declare before you all that my whole life, whether it be long or short, shall be devoted to your service and the service of our great imperial family to which we all belong. But I shall not have the strength to carry out this resolution alone unless you join in it with me, as I now invite you to do. I know that your support will be unfailingly given.

God help me to make good my vow, and God bless all of you who are willing to share in it.

We might find within her realms very many things that do not accord with her character or her wish, but we would not, for that reason, say that she had no right to be called "Queen." Indeed, we feel proud to say that human welfare, the welfare of the people in her dominions, means more to her than the diamonds in her coronation crown. What a change in the concept of royalty has taken place in the last one hundred and fifty years that we can say that! Her queenliness—it is a beautiful word, a Norwegian word that means womanliness—is not denied because here and there conditions exist that are hostile to her wish.

There is a word in the letter to the Hebrews that is relevant here. The anonymous writer of this letter—for it was not Paul and some scholars think it was a woman—says: "We see not yet all things subjected to him, but we behold him . . . crowned with glory and honour" (Heb. 2:8-9). It is though the writer is trying to say: "Not yet, not yet, not yet: there are places in his dominion where all is not in accord with his will, but this does not deny that he reigns." To use a military metaphor, there may be "mopping up" operations still to be done, but the issue is not in doubt. The victory is already won. Paul says that again and again. "He must reign until he has put all his enemies under his feet." He must reign not because of the release of omnipotent force that could not be resisted, but he must reign because right must in the end triumph. That idea is very deep in the human heart, the idea that our human values not only have validity, but have energy so that in the end they will all be justified. Indeed, we have seen this energy at work, and when evil is confronted by his royal power it is seen to be evil and its overthrow is not long delayed. It is not as though we made a list of the evils in the world and then could do nothing but wring our hands, knowing not what to do. When applied courageously Christianity wins. We know the remedy. Love may seem denied by cruelty; kindness may seem feeble, but in the end the royal values win. He *must* reign. Listen to these words of an American Congregational minister (1836—1918):

> I know that right is right
>   And givers shall increase;
> That duty lights the way
>   For the beautiful feet of peace;
> That courage is better than fear
>   And faith is truer than doubt.
> And fierce though the fiends may fight
>   And long though the angels hide,
> I know that truth and right
>   Have the universe on their side,
> And that somewhere beyond the stars
>   Is a Love that is stronger than hate.
> When the night unlocks her bars
>   I shall see Him and I will wait.[2]

[2]*Ultima Veritas* by Washington Gladden. Used by permission of Houghton Mifflin Company.

He *must* reign. There is energy in these values, and they will win, not because God will blot out resistence by irresistible might—for since such violence would defeat purpose, it would express weakness not power—but because gradually men will awaken to the glory and beauty of real values and will insist that they be enthroned in life.

Now that is a very hard thing to say in these days, and my first point was an admittance of those things that seem to deny it. But how small is our faith compared with that of the early Church! To the early Church it must have seemed, from all human accounting of things, as though there were little chance of the Church surviving, let alone winning. If you had seen Pilate on the marble steps of his palace, and you had seen Jesus, pale and wan and weak, and you had been asked, "Which name will last?"—would you have said "Jesus"? Would you really? Wouldn't you have said: "Don't be silly. Pilate is the representative of the all-powerful might of Rome. This man is the leader of an insignificant sect. He is a carpenter himself. His followers have no power. They were customs' clerks and fishermen, and they have all run away. Don't be silly, if one name lasts, it will be that of Pilate. He represents imperial Rome." But history has judged between them. You would never have heard of Pilate had it not been for Jesus. The true royalty was with the Prisoner. We should not speak of the judgment of Jesus. It was the judgment of Pilate, not Jesus.

Who, on the day when Peter was crucified upside down in Rome, would ever have dreamed that today the only ancient building still in use, standing in a city full of the ruins of temples to the ancient gods, is a great cathedral raised to the glory of King Jesus and called the Cathedral Church of St. Peter?

And so throughout the history of the early Church. If

you had seen a deformed tent-maker, with a stammer, called Paul, who suffered from constant physical illness, and was nothing to look at and could not talk, as indeed the New Testament tells you (II Cor. 10:10); if you had seen him standing on Mars Hill, of all places, in Athens, the center of the world's culture, and if you had been asked, "Which will last—the culture of Athens or the poor talking of this funny little man?"—you would not have been in any doubt. You and I would probably have laughed with the others. Athens sneered him out of the city. But history has judged between them. "He must reign until he hath put all his enemies under his feet" because developing man will honor the royal values and give them the place they deserve in his life, and it is because of that vision that we can work with such confidence and optimism.

3. First the sneer; then the vision, and then, last, the challenge. There must be loyalty to a king. My friend, Dr. John Whale, frequently speaks of "the Crown Rights of the Redeemer." Loyalty to a king means getting his will done wherever it can be done. In an earthly kingdom the state has enough power to assert this will. In a kingdom of love it is going to depend on the response of loving hearts. Christ depends on us.

I remember Dr. Fosdick of New York, whom I very greatly love and admire, speaking words which stung me to action, as they were meant to do. He said:

We have not failed to set Christ in the light of beauty, but we have failed to set him in the light of duty. Jesus did not say, "Worship me"; he said, "Follow me." A great soul does not want his ego idolized; he wants his cause supported.

We set him in the stained-glass window, wearing a crown; we sing hymns about him like "Crown Him with

Many Crowns," and we show him respect in our ceremonies, in our anthems, in our litanies, and in our creeds, and we call him "King." Poetry praises him and music lifts his name to the skies, *but these can become ways of dismissing him.* Do we set him in the light of action? Are we trying to win new subjects for this King, and are we, in any sphere or life that is open to us, trying to get his will done?

In Edinburgh some time ago there a conference of nearly two thousand young people, and by chance there happened to be a similar gathering of the same organization and on the same date meeting in Japan. The authorities from the Japanese meeting sent a cable to the youngsters who were meeting in the great hall in Edinburgh, and in a hushed silence the cable from Japan was read to the meeting, and this is what it said: "Let us make Jesus King." Thrilling! But how much more thrilling if half a dozen statesmen of various nations that you and I are thinking about came to that conclusion. Make Jesus King! What a new way would open for this bewildered and problem-troubled, baffled world if those whose voices are heard throughout the world and whose decisions make a difference to treaties and to legislation, would adopt that slogan sent from Japan some years ago to a gathering of young people! Make Jesus King!

Let us work for it! Let us do all we can for it, and let us begin now with an act first of abdication, and then of coronation! We could do the two acts at once by saying, and meaning, two lines in one of our hymns.

> Rule over me, Lord Jesus,
> And make my heart Thy throne.

Dare I fondly hope that he will effectively rule the world if even my heart, which I pretend to have given him, is often divided in its loyalty and sometimes is in open rebellion against its King? By our daily submission and by our daily loyalty we can help the King to come into his own, and we can hasten the fulfillment of an ancient prophecy: "The kingdoms of this world shall become the kingdoms of our God and of his Christ, and he shall reign for ever and ever."

VIII

The Door and the Way

[Jesus said,] I am the door.—JOHN 10:9
I am the way.—JOHN 14:6

"I AM the door: by me if any man enter in, he shall be saved, and shall go in and go out, and find pasture" (K.J.V.).

If, in imagination we go straight to Palestine and meditate for a few moments on the closing scenes in the daily life of a shepherd in our Lord's day, our text will light up at once with meaning and beauty.

We must remember that in the East, now, as in the days of long ago, the shepherd goes in front of his sheep, leading them, not driving them from behind as is the case in the West.

Let us imagine that it is evening. As the sun is setting and the shadows lengthen, we can see the shepherd coming over the shoulder of the hill, making for the sheepfold down in the valley.

The sheepfold must be described. It consists of four high, rough walls surmounted by thorns fixed along the top so as to keep out the thief and the robber who might climb up some other way (John 10:1). In one of the walls, the one nearest the stream that threads its way through the valley, there is a space a little wider than a man's body. The shepherd, preceding the sheep, stands in that gap facing outwards, and he calls his sheep to him by name as they come toward him over the hillside. One of the most impressive and lovely things which you can still see in Palestine is the way in which, if two flocks of sheep intermingle while the shepherds are chatting or eating, a shepherd with the utmost ease can separate them without any use of dogs or of chasing the sheep about. He stands a little above them on the hillside and simply calls them to him by name (John 10:3).

Let us imagine the first sheep approaching the shepherd. It is the leader, a strong healthy animal. The shepherd, however, looks it over carefully for some brier may be clinging to its fleece and cause it subsequent discomfort. Then, satisfied that all is well, the shepherd turns his body sideways so that the sheep may move past him into the fold. The shepherd literally is the door, and when the sheep has passed by him it is safe (John 10:9).

The next sheep has bruised its head on a rock perhaps, or it has been butted by another. Then the shepherd takes his horn of oil and gently massages it into the bruised head. We remember the sentence in the shepherd psalm: "Thou hast anointed my head with oil" (23:5).

The sheepfold is placed in that position so that the nearby stream, running through the valley, can be trapped into a large stone two-handled cup. The water runs into the cup and out again—"My cup runneth over." Stephen Haboush, who was a shepherd for many years on these very hills, has explained that a sheep is frightened of turbulent water. A rushing stream can carry a frightened sheep down stream and drown it, its thick fleece, if sodden, making it hard for the sheep to spring out of the water, hence the sentence: "He leadeth me beside *the still waters*."[1]

---

[1] Stephen Haboush, the author of *My Shepherd Life in Galilee*, was passing through Texas and attended this lecture when it was given there, and in conversation with him I was able to confirm my own observations, made when I was in Palestine in 1934, and to check my facts.

Here is a sheep approaching now that looks very jaded and out of sorts. The shepherd lifts the big stone cup brimming full with water. By lifting it the water is quiet and the sheep drinks more readily. When the sheep is refreshed the shepherd turns his body again and the sheep passes into the fold.

Now all the sheep are folded. The shepherd does not rely on any temporary hurdle or gate to close the entrance. He builds in the gap a huge fire, with himself on the inside, near the sheep. Then, crouching over the fire, he eats his evening meal, watching over his flocks by night. Finally, having made up the fire he wraps himself in his cloak, and with his feet to the fire he lies down near the sheep. Their bleating slowly ceases and, as the stars shine out, the shepherd may rest, as the sheep do, in perfect safety. Wild animals may be in evidence. Indeed the cry of the hyena and the jackal and even the wolf may still be heard. But wild animals are terrified of fire. They cannot jump the high walls, crested with thorns, and in the gateway between the wolf and the sheep is not only the fire, but *the body of the shepherd*.

Tomorrow at dawn the shepherd will lead them out again, and in that rhythm they spend their days going in and going out. But in every experience the shepherd is with them.

I think the lovely picture has much to teach us. We who try to follow Christ, the Door and the Way, must learn that rhythm. There is the going in and going out; in to the quiet hours of meditation and rest and refreshment, and then out, adventuring perhaps far and wide, and yet safe in both going in and going out as long as we do not stray from the Shepherd; into the fold with God's other sheep and then out to witness in the world. We have a sense of security because we are in Christ's care, but a sense of freedom because the whole world is our pasture. Much could be said about the rhythm of the Christian life in which we can err if we are "in" too much or "out" too much.

But I wish to focus our thought more on the ideas conveyed to us by the words "door" and "way." To do this let us look back at the world into which Jesus came with these liberating words. Indeed, what a Liberator he was! He came, he said, quoting Isaiah, "to proclaim release to the captives, . . . to set at liberty them that are bruised." And he added, "Today hath this scripture been fulfilled in your ears" (Luke 4:18-21).

The world to which he came was a world in chains. Men groaned under their burdens. We complain of our taxation, but Jesus' father paid a water tax, a city tax, a meat tax, a salt tax, a house tax, and a road tax. Roman tyrants could exact tribute to Caesar, compel a man to carry a burden, lend his cloak, and accompany any Roman traveler on a journey, however dangerous and uncongenial.

The ecclesiastical tyranny imposed by the Pharisees—their own countrymen—was just as irksome. Meticulous ceremonial observances had to be carried out. Some of the details make one laugh now, but it was no laughing matter then. It must have been infuriating and exasperating. That it should ever be linked with the word "religion," that ever man should impose it on his fellows and pretend that the loving Father, the holy God, cared about such trivial nonsense, accounts in part for the blazing and scathing words that Jesus used about the Pharisees. The measure of the fierceness of his invective was the measure of the tyranny they imposed and of their refusal to understand.

For instance, one must not wear false teeth on the

Sabbath, for to do that is to carry a burden; a woman might wear a ribbon on her gown if it were sewn in—if only pinned in, that, if you please, was carrying a burden. A man must not journey more than a certain distance on the Sabbath, but if, the night before, he went to the prescribed limit and concealed a morsel of food at that point he could call that point his lodging and so travel a new "Sabbath day's journey" beyond it. A woman must not use a mirror on the Sabbath, for if she espied a white hair, she might pluck it out and so fall into the sin of "reaping" on the Sabbath.

With this background, can we not feel and see what a new way Christ opened up; what a door he unfastened? The outward life of the people was hedged round with tiresome Roman restrictions; their inner life hedged round with stupid Jewish ceremonial laws. Christ opened a door into freedom and joy and liberty. Religion was a way of life, and a way of life with God as Father and Friend; putting Caesar in a new perspective of relative unimportance and making religion a relationship with a God, all-Wise, all-Loving, purposeful and powerful, one who alone *mattered*.

Again and again I find myself coming back to the beginning of Christianity. Let us do so again now. Let us remember that Christianity began with a handful of simple people trying to learn how to live, and believing, when they met him, that Jesus was a Door and a Way to life.

I believe he chose men like Peter and James and John and Andrew because their minds were open to new ideas. Their thoughts were able to take new shape. The ecclesiastics were far too rigid, too stereotyped, too set in their ceremonies and conventions and restrictions to be able to respond to the revolutionary ideas of Christ.

The first followers of Jesus were not outstandingly clever people and certainly were not wealthy or of high social standing, but they could love and they could change their ideas. When they looked at Jesus I think they felt: "This is what God meant human life to be like. This is true religion. Here is the secret of the mystery of the art of life."

Are not men seeking this Way today? Is not the unrest of our time due mainly to the fact that the art of victorious living eludes us? Thinking people do not expect life to be a long experience of facile happiness, but they do expect life to make sense. They don't imagine that they can find a solution to every problem, but they want a basis of certainty from which they can project a faith that there *is* a solution. They are not blind to the difficulties of the Church, but they have the right to expect that the Church will respond to their need, that its services will be relevant to the problems they meet, that they will not be put off by meaningless formulae, or asked to give intellectual assent to unexamined and unexplained propositions which, as far as they understand them at all, seem either incredible or unimportant. No one likes to have his mind doped by pious phrases that could have any one of a dozen meanings.

So nearly two thousand years ago men and women banded themselves together to try out this new way of life. They were repeatedly called indeed "the men of the way" (Acts 9:2; 19:9, 23; 22:4; 24:14, 22). They suffered and were persecuted, but they had an underlying joy and a philosophy of life that made them ignore their own troubles—which God, they felt, would handle for them—and be much more concerned about other people.

They didn't worry much about what they believed. The young Church had no set creeds for three hundred years, and even then only wrote them down to rebut the attacks made on them. Their creed grew up out of their experience and we should be wise to love God and our neighbor and keep very close to Christ and let our creed take shape, not trying to force it into accepted channels, but concentrating on loving and praying and meditating, so that belief will follow experience just as it does when a man falls in love with a woman. He doesn't begin with a creed about her. He thinks, "I would like to share her life if she will have me," and his beliefs about her grow up out of his experience. Is Christianity in its early stages very different from falling in love with Christ, sharing life with him, trying out his way of living? When I asked the Chaplain General of all Her Majesty's Forces what was the gist of his message to the men, he replied very simply: "I want them to fall in love with Jesus Christ."

Clearly it is incumbent on us to commend this Way to others. Many seem unable to find any door into a fuller and more satisfying way of living.

The kind of burglar of the soul who asks you whether you are saved, just as you want to get a nap in the corner of a railway coach, is fortunately becoming extinct. It should be remembered that a religious witness, and indeed an invitation to another to follow our Christian way of life, should frequently begin a long way from the use of religious jargon. The invitation, "Come to Jesus," doesn't make sense to a large number of people. Appeals to "surrender the life to Christ" can be nauseating, superior, and repellent. But everyone understands good humor, good will, and the kindly deed. Sometimes the most religious thing we can do in a situation is to keep the conversation off religion. Jesus

THE AUTOBIOGRAPHY OF JESUS

didn't say to Zacchaeus: "Brother, are you saved?" He said: "May I come and have dinner with you?" The prodigal's return was not celebrated by a service but by roast veal, and the story ends not with a prayer meeting, but a dance.

When Dick Sheppard was visiting some troops, the chaplain pointed out one soldier and said to Dick: "I can't get near him at all. Religion doesn't interest him and I can make no impression on him." Dick and the soldier were seen together later in animated conversation. The chaplain was astonished and asked Dick the secret. "I should be glad, Dr. Sheppard," he said pompously, "if you would explain what religious approach you make to a person who seems entirely indifferent to religion." "Religion," said Dick, with his lovable twinkle, "I didn't talk religion. I told him two funny stories and then asked after his mother"!—But isn't that the right approach to religion? Good humor, good will, caring—these make a bridge and only after such a bridge is built can the traffic of more intimate religion pass. The pope is called the pontiff, or the bridgemaker. In some sense we must all be pontiffs. Blessed are the bridgemakers. A bridgehead so often establishes the kingdom of heaven against its enemies.

We simply must not try to impose our views on other people. We must do the same jobs as other people do and meet the same difficulties and face the same suffering—for religion is no insurance against trouble—and do all and meet all with those qualities that spring from a close communion with the Master, thinking more of others' troubles than of our own. That's the WAY to win people. Christians should "have a WAY with them," seeking, in the lovely language of St. Francis' prayer: "Not so much to be loved as to love, not so much to be consoled as to console, not so much to be understood as to understand."

Hundreds of people wistfully seek a way. The tragedy

is they don't believe the Church knows the way either, so they go on in their frustration, their loneliness, their unhappiness, never feeling quite well, never knowing radiance of spirit, hating to be alone, filling every possible moment with some triviality or other, lest the cloud of their condition should cover the whole sky of consciousness and leave them in panic and despair. Their condition is a challenge to every one of us to deepen his communion with Christ, so that we may influence the world as the early Church did. We must be men of the Way, until, while men are too reticent to say so, they may know in their hearts that we have a secret, the clue to life's meaning and purpose and joy, and turn and find their way to his feet.

Last, this one point. There is never any situation, believe me, from which Jesus Christ cannot find the way out. The Way! The Door! If you go in, he will show you the way out. "I am the Door: by me if any man enter in, he shall be saved, and shall go in and go out, and find pasture." Perhaps you don't know which way to turn. In some difficult situation you don't know what to do. He comes to you and says: "I am the Way. I will find the way out for you." You have only to be quiet for half an hour and look at him and listen. You will know which way to turn.

I was reading recently about a famous picture in which the artist sought to depict that great interview between Faust and Satan. Faust gambled for his soul, and the artist depicts the two sitting at a chessboard, the Devil on one side and Faust on the other. In this picture the face of the Devil leers with glee because he thinks he has got Faust completely at his mercy and completely beaten. I don't understand the game of chess, but I am told that if you look at the picture it does look as if the situation is checkmate. Faust looks crumbled up and beaten. The Devil gloats in superiority. One day a master of chess was studying the picture in the gallery where it hangs. He looked at it and looked at it, and then, to the surprise of everybody else in the art gallery, he shouted out: "It's a lie! The king and the knight can move!"

Yes, Jesus is the King. You are his knight. There is another move. He knows that move. It is a lie to say: "There isn't a way out. I am beaten." There is another move. Have you ever been in a situation and known the comfort of just that, that there is a way out? Imagine that you and I are lost in a jungle at night. We don't know which way to turn. We stumble about in the darkness. We trip over the roots, blunder through the undergrowth, get our faces lashed by the low boughs of the trees. All through the night it goes on until we are in agony, frantic with fear. Then, as the dawn comes you shout to me and say: "I can see a road." The inexpressible comfort of knowing that there is a way! A traveler friend of mine, who on one occasion was actually and literally lost, said to me: "When I saw the road I could have knelt down and kissed it." Exactly! The situation in one way is not very different. When you find Christ you may still be in the jungle, but what a difference in your heart! You are not at the end of the journey, but you are at the end of your wandering, at the end of looking for a way. There is a way home. Jesus says that to you *now*. "Come with me! Try my way of life! I am the way!"

A poor man hung on a cross and thought that there was no way, that this was the end, deluded fanatic as he was. And he turned to Jesus, and Jesus said: "Today thou shalt be with me in Paradise." Is it fanciful to end the chapter more or less where we began it, by saying

that the body of the Good Shepherd turned, and
behold, a door, a door into Paradise? My brother, you
can find it too. "I am the door: by me if any man enter in
he shall be saved." Yes, saved, for no one is lost who
knows the way home.

IX

Master and Lord

Ye call me Master and Lord: and ye say well; for so I am.—JOHN 13:13

IF we ask what Jesus is claiming for himself by the use of these two words—presuming that these were words he actually used[1]—the answer *may* simply be that by the word "Master" he meant "Teacher," and that by "Lord" he meant "the Lord of slaves."[2] We must remember that the Fourth Gospel was written many years after the epistles of Paul and that the writer of the Gospel was probably familiar with the epistles. At any rate he would be familiar with the language of Christian usage at that period. The title "Lord," therefore, which became the favorite appellation for Christ among the earliest Christians, and was the word used for God in the Greek version of the Old Testament—the "Bible" on which many of the first Christians had been brought up[3]— would not be used to convey in the later Gospel less than it certainly meant to the early Christians who read Paul's epistles, namely, one who stood in a unique relationship with God and must be regarded, not merely as a human Messiah, but as a divine Son of God. Certainly, by the time people read the Fourth Gospel, the word "Lord"

[1] It is difficult in the Fourth Gospel to decide how much is the actual language of Jesus and how much is the interpretation of a devout mind. Scholars are agreed that the first three Gospels are nearer our Lord's actual language than is the fourth. But see pp. 7-10.

[2] William Temple, *Readings in St. John's Gospel.*

[3] Frederic Greeves, *Jesus, the Son of God,* and *An Approach to Christian Doctrine.*

would have come to mean far more than "owner of slaves," and in their minds would scarcely be devalued to its earlier meaning.

Let us look briefly at the picture. The room is all ready for the Last Supper. It is to take place in the large upper room built on the flat roof of Mark's father's house. Mark's father and mother, we may assume, have prepared it themselves. The meal was secret. We note the secret preparations and the signal of the man carrying the pitcher of water.[4] Had the preparations not been secret the room would have been buzzing with servants and the incident we are to look at would never have happened; a slave would have met each guest at the doorway, or more probably as he lay reclining on his couch, would have unfastened his sandals and bathed his feet. But since the meal was secret, no slave was allowed to wait on the guests. Mark or his parents probably carried in the food themselves. The water and basin and towel—the water perhaps in the very pitcher to which reference has been made—were provided.

The disciples entered in ones and twos so as not to attract notice. Luke tells us that even within the upper room they quarreled as to who should be greatest (Luke 22:24). There was no slave to carry out the usual courtesies, and not one of them would stoop to do it. It was the most menial task of all. To do *that* would certainly be to lose the claim to greatness. So we can see them, like sulky schoolboys, without even the humor to laugh at the situation—the unthinkable situation in the East—of reclining at table with all the discomfort, let alone the ceremonial defilement, of unwashed feet, with the filth and ordure of the Eastern street between the toes. There they reclined with burning, angry faces, flushed with

[4]Mark 14:13. A clever signal, for women usually carried water, yet the signal was not so extraordinary as to draw attention, for a man's wife might be too ill, or away from home, or the man might be a widower or bachelor.

their argument, each one of them determined that *he* was not going to be the one to acknowledge himself servant of all.

Then "during supper" (not "after supper") Jesus rose from his place. I think he waited for supper to begin because not till then would the kindly host withdraw and leave them to the privacy they wanted. Jesus, unwilling to shame his men, waited till the host had withdrawn. Then he removed his outer robe, took a towel, and pouring water into a basin began to wash his disciples' feet—began to do the menial task which not one of his men would undertake.

When the lovely, acted parable was concluded, Jesus said:

Know ye what I have done to you? Ye call me Master and Lord: and ye say well; for so I am. If I then, your Lord and Master, have washed your feet; ye also ought to wash one another's feet. (K.J.V.)

It was an acted parable to teach humility, to reveal that greatness is always characterized by humility. Indeed, it is a revelation of the nature of God himself. When God deals with men, he does not—so to speak—throw his weight about, and is eager not to dominate, or impress, or overwhelm, but to serve in utter lowliness of mind. God is like that. The narrative of the foot washing opens with an amazing sentence: "Jesus, knowing that the Father had given all things into his hands, and that he came forth from God, and goeth unto God, . . . began to wash the disciples' feet." How different it is from all human ideas of majesty and power! We might have read: "Jesus, knowing that he came from God and went to God, began to assert his divinity, demand men's adoration, receive their worship, and establish his authority." Instead he undertakes the lowliest and most menial and despised task, not as one who merely teaches a lesson, but as one who, in such a deed, reveals his own nature and is most truly himself. So Schweitzer—one of the greatest men of our age, if not *the* greatest—though he is a Nobel prize winner, a great philosopher, a great musician, and a great theologian, is seen treating the leprous sores of unknown African villagers, not just because the news camera is ready to take his photo, but because he thus expresses his own nature and that of his Master. If we believe—as I do—that Jesus, "coming from the depths of God's Being,"[5] possessing in himself the very nature of Deity, was revealing the essential nature of divinity, then indeed we must correct many of our ideas about God. God's nature is not so eloquently set forth in acts of overwhelming omnipotence as in those of lowly service. None of the words beginning with "omni" describes the *essence* of Deity. The virtues that men can share with God, like love and humility, are nearer the essence of Deity than these. He that is really great is the servant of all.

There is another thought that we must notice, though I will not here dwell upon it. I am convinced that the foot-washing incident was part of a significant series of events which took place on the night before Good Friday, all of which were connected into an acted parable portraying our Lord's spiritual "marriage" to his people, or, if you like, to the Church.[6] For the early Christians the Church was often pictured as "the bride" (Rev. 21:2), or as "the wife of the Lamb" (Rev. 21:9). Note the following similarities.

1. A Jewish wedding ceremony started by the bride-groom going to the bride's home. Jesus was frequently

[5] A phrase used by Vincent Taylor.

[6] I have worked it out fully in *A Plain Man Looks at the Cross* (Abingdon Press).

referred to as the Bridegroom (Matt. 9:15; Mark 2:19; Luke 5:34; cf. Matt. 25:1-13) who came to earth to seek his bride.

> From heaven He came and sought her
> To be His holy bride.

2. According to Jewish ceremony, the bridegroom then brought the bride to his own home, and his first act was to stoop ånd wash her feet. Says Dr. J. A. Findlay: "Jesus washed His disciples' feet to make them worthy successors of the true Israel, the *bride* of God."

3. In a Jewish wedding the foot washing is followed by the feast. In that "large upper room, richly furnished," Jesus ate a Passover feast with his disciples. It is noteworthy that Jesus thought of the Last Supper as a special Passover. "With desire," he said; "I have desired to eat this passover with you" (Luke 22:15). Now the Jews always regarded the Passover as a kind of marriage between God and Israel. The Passover celebration opened with the words, "Behold the *Bridegroom* cometh!"—and indeed many passages of Old Testament scripture bear out this idea of God as the Husband of Israel.[7]

4. In a Jewish wedding the feast is followed by the words of the marriage covenant. Jesus after the supper gave to his men the words of a "new *covenant*" (Luke 22:20).

Paul and John in many phrases speak of Jesus as the Bridegroom and of the Church as the Bride (Rev. 21:2; Eph. 5:23-25; II Cor. 11:2 [Moffatt]). One feels sure that by the time the Fourth Gospel was written the early Christians had seen the significance of the foot-washing incident not only as an example of humility, but as an acted parable of the marriage of Christ to his Church by

[7]Consider Jer. 2:2; 31:31; Hos. 2:2-20.

which he pledged himself to stand by it "for better for worse, for richer for poorer," and redeem it, until he could present the Bride to God without "spot or wrinkle or any such thing; . . . holy and without blemish" (Eph. 5:27).

These considerations make me feel that the word "Lord" in this context must have meant far more to the readers of the Fourth Gospel than the "Lord of slaves," and much more than the mere title, "Sir," which one could call the minimum meaning which the word carries in other contexts.[8]

The question we must face is one which often crops up and puzzles people. Should we call Jesus God? Is he divine in any sense different from that in which we speak of all men having a "divine spark" within them? Men ask: "If Christ were God, what was happening to the government of the universe while God was confined in a body that lived in Palestine?" They say: "If Christ were God he would not have prayed, for it would have been talking to himself." They say: "If he were God, he wasn't man; if he were man, he wasn't God. Each excludes the other."

For myself, I can only admit readily that the nature of Christ is a great mystery, and though I shall try to answer some questions, there is, for me, a reverent area of mystery containing many problems, the answer to which I simply do not know. Nor have I ever found anyone who claims to banish all mystery and answer all the questions.

For years I used to think of Christ as a very good man around whom legends of divinity had gathered, but who, though far removed from even the greatest saints, was yet in the same category. I was gradually, but

[8] E.g. Matt. 8:2; 9:28; 14:30; 24:46; 25:37; Mark 9:24; 10:51; Luke 9:57; 11:1; 17:5; 23:42; John 6:68; 8:11; 9:36, etc.

irresistibly, pushed, however, to the conclusion that he was and is unique and that the word "human," though true, is not big enough to contain the truth about him. I think that in the days of his flesh, he *felt* human and was sometimes puzzled that no one else had similar powers. Did his question "Whom say men that I am?" arise when he was puzzled about himself? I believe that he had to fight temptation and difficulty with no other weapons than are available to us—else he was not truly human—but that he stood in a unique relationship with God, revealed God in a unique way and had a unique control of energies belonging to a supernormal level of being, as yet—at any rate—strange to us. When every allowance is made for possible accretions to the stories of his deeds, accretions made of magic, I cannot avoid the conclusion that he worked miracles which have never been repeated;—the Resurrection for instance. He seemed at home in a different world from ours, and the energies which belong to that realm he used as we use the energies of the physical world in which we are at home.

When men ask what was happening to the universe if God was confined in a body that lived in Palestine, I think the answer is that "confined" is not an apposite word. If it were, then, with Nestorius, we could speak of God being "eight days old" at Bethlehem, which is nonsense. God added to all his other creative activities that of incarnation in Christ. By that incarnation I mean that God was in Christ to a maximum fullness consonant with humanity, that God dwelt in Christ as fully as God can dwell in man without disrupting and destroying his real humanity. Christ thus was not omniscient or omnipresent or omnipotent, but at the same time he revealed the essential nature of God as fully as human nature can reveal it. In any case deity is more importantly revealed in terms of love than in terms of

112

power, or knowledge, or omnipresence. The New Testament makes it clear that human nature involved a subordination, so that the incarnate Son prayed to his Father and sought his Father's will, but yet there remained a unity between them which places the Son outside the category of the merely human.

I should like to set down here the considerations which have compelled me to feel that the word "human" is not big enough to describe all Christ was and is. To me, he is not only Master, but Lord; not only human Teacher, but divine Saviour; not only the highest expression of the nature of man, but the fullest expression of the essential nature of God. I know that the nature of God is beyond the reach of any man's mind, but Christ is as much of God as I can fathom. The nature of God is as far greater than human nature can express as the ocean is greater than a cupful taken from a wave breaking on the seashore. Yet the quality is the same, say of transparency and chemical content. I am told that color may go far beyond violet and ultraviolet at one end of the spectrum and beyond red and infrared at the other, but the colors between are all that I can *see*. Jesus is the spectrum of God. The rest is speculation. I believe Jesus lives still in the unseen, that he has taken our humanity into his divine nature and is "Brother Man" for us forever, as well as Pre-existent Son of God, "begotten of His Father before all worlds, . . . True God of true God, . . . who for us men and for our salvation came down from heaven."

1. Consider first his attitude to sin. He gave his followers the idea that he was sinless. Says John: "He was manifested to take away sins, and in him is no sin" (I John 3:5). The author of the Fourth Gospel reports that he challenged his disciples: "Which of you convicteth me of sin?" (8:46). It is a question no subsequent writer

would have invented. "When *ye* pray," he said, "say Forgive *us*," as if he himself stood apart needing no forgiveness. He spoke of "my Father and your Father" (John 20:17), as if there were a difference in relationship, and only to the disciples said: "When *ye* pray, say *Our* Father." Says H. R. Mackintosh:

> On every page of the Gospel we encounter such imperial demands for obedience as well as gracious promises of help and pardon, as it would have been an enormity for a sinful man to utter.[9]

This attitude is so different from that of even the greatest saints. The greater their saintliness the more sensitive they are to sin, the more conscious they are of imperfection. So even Paul talks of himself as in danger of being cast away though he has preached to others (I Cor. 9:27). He feels unworthy to be called an apostle (I Cor 15:9) and cries out in mental agony: "O wretched man that I am! who shall deliver me out of the body of this death?" (Rom. 7:24). His sins seem as foul and offensive as the corpse strapped to the back of a prisoner by a pagan and horrible custom, a "body of death" from which by no effort of his own could the criminal escape. But Jesus can quietly say: "Which of you convicteth me of sin?"

Indeed, Jesus even appears to forgive sin. No wonder the scribes called him blasphemous, and ask: "Who can forgive sins but one, even God?" Any merely human person would have interrupted here to say: "You must not confuse me with God." Yet Jesus made no interruption. He assumed the prerogative of God. He did not merely state that the man was forgiven. *He forgave him:*

---

[9]*The Doctrine of the Person of Christ.*

That ye may know that the Son of man hath authority on earth to forgive sins (he saith to the sick of the palsy), I say unto thee, Arise, take up thy bed, and go unto thy house. (Mark 2:7, 10-11 A.S.V.)

A convincing proof to me that Jesus reacted in a unique way in regard to sin is the fact that we would not willingly allow anyone to imagine that we were sinless. Having sinned, it would be hypocrisy for us to deal with another as though we had not. When we seek to help others, it is as fellow sinners. If someone so grievously misunderstood us as to imagine that we stood in some special relationship to God, how quickly we would disillusion him. Yet the Jews sought to kill him *because he made himself equal with God* (John 5:18). According to the Fourth Gospel, he called himself "the Son of God" (10:36), and when the scribes charged him with blasphemy for doing so, he asked them why they called that blasphemy. To deny the blasphemy was to assert divinity. If the incident is literal history, it is a declaration of divinity in six words: "I am the Son of God." Even though this phrase was sometimes used for a very good man, as in Mark 15:39, yet in the context of the rest of the passage it connotes more. The author of the Fourth Gospel tells us plainly that the whole Gospel was written to prove that Jesus was the Son of God (20:30-31).

All this adds up to something outside the category of the "merely human."

2. Consider, secondly, the words he used himself. This book studies each of the sayings of Christ which contains the phrase: "I am." They are so startling that one is driven to the conclusion that the speaker is either mad or divine. Who among all the sons of men could say that when men had seen him, they had seen God? (John

14:9). What mere man could say: "I am the Light of the world," "I am the Bread of life," "I am the Way, the Truth, and the Life," "I am the Resurrection and the Life"? Who could assert that twelve legions of angels were at his disposal? (Matt. 26:53). Who could speak of the glory he had with God before the world was (John 17:5), or say, "Before Abraham was, I am"—another significant "I am"? Who could prophesy his resurrection *and make the prophecy come true?* Who could assert that his gospel would be preached throughout the whole world? (Matt. 26:13). Who could make such demands on human nature as to say that he came before the claims of family, even of husband and wife (Matt. 10:37); that by their attitude to him man would be finally judged (John 12:47); that heaven and earth would pass away, but his words would remain and be vindicated? (Mark 13:31). Who, dying in agony, could *promise,* not hope, to meet in Paradise a poor dying wretch on the cross next to his own? (Luke 23:43). It is madness for a mere man to pose as one whose unique function it was to introduce other men to God (Matt. 11:27; Luke 10:22).

Yet, if this be madness, it is the most attractive insanity the world has ever seen, and its paradox must ever be that if it spread it would bring sanity to this mad world as nothing else has the power to do. I cannot conceive that any board of psychiatrists could sit down and study the Gospels, find in our Lord the symptoms of psychosis, and solemnly write him a certificate of lunacy. To me the alternative is that here we have someone who has all the values of God which a human life can express. He spoke like God. He made the claims that God makes. He did what God does. He knew God in a unique way.

3. A third consideration arises. It is the evidence of those nearest to him, those who knew him best, and

those who knew about him from eyewitnesses. There could scarcely have been people less willing to accord divinity to a man than the Jews. "Hear, O Israel: the Lord our God is one Lord" (Deut. 6:4). All their religion stemmed from that basic truth. Monotheism was an essential part of the Jewish religion. That a man should be worshiped was to a Jew incredibly blasphemous.

Now during the days of his flesh before the Resurrection, it is doubtful whether Jesus was worshiped. We find the word "worship" used in regard to him,[10] but the word could, and probably did, mean the bowing of the knee in reverence. When, for example, we read that a leper "worshipped him," we should probably translate: "did obeisance to him." Yet, I suspect that even before his death, his disciples, monotheists to a man, began to feel that the word "man" was too small to hold him. Says Dr. Maltby in a beautiful sentence, "When they said their prayers to God at night, there was another face on the screen of their minds and they fell asleep thinking of Jesus."

But after the Resurrection there is no doubt whatever that Jesus was worshiped in our sense of the word. "My Lord and *my God,*" says Thomas (John 20:28), and is not rebuked for blasphemy. Whatever the historicity of the story, its inclusion shows a current belief. The earliest reference to Christianity in secular literature is found in the Letter of Pliny to Trajan in A.D. 112, and it speaks of certain Jews "who sang hymns to Christ as God." In the First Letter to the Corinthians we find the Aramaic form retained, "Maran atha," which means "Our Lord cometh," or perhaps, "O Lord, come" (I Cor. 16:22). He that was expected was a Divine Being. In the book of

---

[10] Matt. 8:2; 9:18; 14:33; 15:25; 18:26; 20:20; Mark 5:6; 15:19, etc. Matt. 14:33 may mean worship in our sense, but since the Greek word is used in both senses, it is better not to press the point. The parallel in Mark does not settle the matter either way.

Acts we read of Stephen's martyrdom. The dying saint cried out at last: "Behold, I see the heavens opened, and the Son of man standing on the right hand of God," and later, "Lord Jesus, receive my spirit," and later still, "Lord, lay not this sin to their charge" (Acts 7:56, 59, 60). This is, without doubt, as Dr. Temple once said, "a devotional equation of Jesus with the God of the spirits of all flesh."[11]

It is indubitable that Paul spoke of Jesus as, before his conversion, he would have spoken of no one save God. He speaks of Christ's pre-existence (Eph. 1:4; Phil. 2:6), of his part in God's creative activity (Col. 1:15-17), and refers to him continually as God's own Son (Rom. 1:4; 8:3, 32; Gal. 4:4).

It is indubitable that John's Gospel and first epistle make similar claims. Jesus is the only begotten Son (John 3:16) and one with the Father (John 10:30; 14:9). The Gospel is written "that ye may believe that Jesus is the Christ, the Son of God; and that believing ye may have life in his name" (John 20:31).

It would be a bold man who, to assert the claim that Jesus was only a good man, had to ignore the evidence of those who were closest to him, who either knew him or knew those who knew him. Such a person would have to tear up the most significant parts of the New Testament.

The idea of the worship of a man is abhorrent to us all. I remember that when my wife and I parted from a gardener, who had been in our employment in India for six years and of whom we were very fond, he prostrated himself on the platform of the Madras Central Station, tried to hold our ankles and used words which were the language of worship. He persuaded his girl-wife, who was with him, to do the same. I shall never forget the sight of them both, completely prostrate, with their

[11]In *Christus Veritas.*

hands on our shoes. I do not think I have ever been so embarrassed in my life, and though we loved them both dearly, our first act was to raise them to their feet, shake them warmly by the hand and say that though we should always remember them and find our hearts warmed at thought of them, they must never, never regard us as any different from themselves, fellow Christians treading the upward way. We read in the Acts (14:11-15) that when Paul and Barnabas were taken for gods, they were distressed so that "they rent their garments" and cried, "We also are men of like passions with you." It seems to me that no one who was not divine could be worshiped without protest. Yet *Jesus accepted men's worship as his right.*

4. There is a fourth line of evidence to which, in my opinion, insufficient attention has been paid. It is the universal appeal of Jesus. Indeed, it is more than that. It is as though Christ were recognized as peculiarly their own by all races. He is a universal, a cosmic Christ, every man's Saviour.

There is a deep significance in this. Jesus was a Jew, and when we talk to a Jew we rarely become unconscious that we are doing so. Yet how often does a modern Christian remember that Jesus was a Jew? He transcends nationality and religious distinction. When Jesus is preached in India, or China, or Africa, he is as winsome and attractive and lovable to the hearer as if he were an Indian, a Chinese, or an African. Mohammedan missionaries find that Mohammed does not appeal in the far North or the far South, the far East or the far West. It is unlikely that the Indian gods and goddesses would have much attractiveness, say, in America or Britain. Buddhism has a bleak time in the West and Confucianism is all but unknown. Our Master and Lord has been preached in all languages to every nation under heaven, and again and again it is as though men *recognize* him as belonging peculiarly to them. The deeply significant comment of a learned Indian pundit, who heard from a missionary for the first time the story of Jesus, was as follows: "I have known Him all my life and now you have told me His name." The Jesus who knew no racial barrier in the days of his flesh and talked to Greek, or Samaritan, or Syrophoenician, or Roman without any consciousness of racial barrier, expresses his divinity in his appeal to all nations. He seems to make conscious a recognition sleeping in the unconscious minds of men and women of all races. Indeed he claimed: "My house shall be called a house of prayer *for all the nations*" (Mark 11:17). "I, if I be lifted up, will draw *all men* unto me." What an impossible claim that is on the lips of a man! Yet how amazingly true it is of Jesus, Master and Lord of Everyman!

So we must leave the matter with many questions unanswered. What is divinity? Is it in essence the best of humanity raised to the nth degree of love and holiness? What is deity? Is that something different, or does it signify the difference between the divinity of Jesus and of all others? Did his divinity or deity give Jesus advantages over "merely human" people, or did it not rather involve added dangers and stresses terrible to him—as terrible as Gethsemane suggests—but unknowable to us? I cannot answer all your questions about Christ for I do not know what the word "deity" connotes. I do not even know what the word "humanity" connotes.

I do know that to me he is human and knowable and lovable, my Master and Teacher and Example. But I know also that he is far, far more than all this, a Divine Friend who is pledged to stand by me, a Divine Saviour who is my only hope of the spiritual attainment for which in my best moments I long, a Divine Judge too good to let me off, too faithful to let me down, too loving to let me go; and how I need a Judge who stands above the superficial fallible judgments of men! Many people fear what is called the "day of judgment." Little do they realize that it will be the happiest day of their lives for they will be understood for the first time. And no one who is not both divine and human can understand man fully.

A friend once told me of an agnostic scientist who was studying ants, so he kept a colony of them under glass, to watch. While marveling at their intelligence and industry and orderliness, he detected a weakness in intelligence. A scout ant discovered food and led others to the spot. Later food was placed in a new position and nearer the nest. This was discovered only by first traveling along the original route, and then on, round the table to the new pile. The professor hoped they would be intelligent enough to take a new short cut—but no! He even built obstacles to divert them, but these they laboriously surmounted, crawled round and over, and so persisted in their original route. "How stupid they are! How I wish I could tell them! If only I could become an ant and show them," said the scientist, "but then, of course, on becoming an ant I should only have an ant's limited intelligence. I should have to become both ant *and* man! Then flashed into his mind a phrase once heard long ago: "Truly God—Truly man."

I cannot quibble as to whether he should be called "the Son of God," or "the Supreme Revelation of God," or "the Word made flesh," or "the Incarnation of God." Men may call him "Avatar" or "Logos," or what they will. For me no "merely human" category is big enough to hold him. The rest is for me a reverent, speculative agnosticism. "If divine truth," said Augustine, "were not too large for our understanding, it would be too small for our hearts." But without violence to my intellectual processes I can call him, with all the fullness of connotation in the New Testament, "Master and Lord." With all my being hushed and awed and bowed in adoration, I can sing one of the oldest hymns of the Christian faith:

> Thou art the King of glory, O Christ!
> Thou art the Everlasting Son of the Father!

X

The Resurrection and
the Life

Jesus said . . . I am the resurrection and the life.
—JOHN 14:6

IN the chapter entitled "The Bread of Life" we thought a little about the nature of life, and the part which Christ plays in imparting the highest kind of life to us. Now I wish to concentrate on the words Jesus is said to have spoken to a bereaved woman at the graveside of her brother.

News has been received that Lazarus is ill. Jesus says: "Our friend Lazarus is fallen asleep; but I go, that I may awake him out of sleep" (John 11:11). Jesus apparently uses a word for "sleep" which might mean either sleep or death.[1] Supposing him to be referring to natural sleep, the disciples conclude that sleep is the best thing possible for the patient. "Lord, if he has fallen asleep, he will recover." So Jesus uses a different word about which there can be no ambiguity. "Lazarus is dead."

Martha's sublime faith is worth our notice as we read the story again—a story, it may be noted, which is only found in this Gospel. "Lord, if thou hadst been here, my brother had not died. And *even now I know that, whatsoever thou shalt ask of God, God will give thee.*" What a tribute that is to our Lord and what a tribute the words, "I know," are to her own faith in him! Jesus replies to this with the promise: "Thy brother shall rise again."

---

[1] Unlike the word he used about Jairus' daughter when he said: "She is not dead but *sleepeth.*" This word is never used for death, and it is strange that men have insisted that Jesus raised a dead girl when Jesus insisted that she was not dead.

Martha, with another "I know," discloses her faith again: "I know that he shall rise again in the resurrection at the last day." Then comes our Lord's shattering statement:

I am the resurrection, and the life: he that believeth on me, though he die, yet shall he live: and whosoever liveth and believeth on me shall never die. Believest thou this?

Martha makes another superb answer, "Yea, Lord: I have believed that thou art the Christ, the Son of God, even he that cometh into the world."

The triumphant ending of the story, with the beloved Lazarus risen and returned to the bosom of his family, I will not dwell on here. Some critics feel that they cannot accept it. Certainly the difficulties are great. Luke was a doctor and would have been thrilled by such a happening. It is strange that it eluded him and that neither he, nor Matthew, nor Mark, says a word about it in those Gospels which were all written much earlier than the fourth. If the next life is all that is claimed for it, what a terrible sentence it was on Lazarus to make him return in order to fortify his sisters' faith:

Oh dreadful is the check, intense the agony—
When the ear begins to hear, the eyes begin to see;
When the pulse begins to throb, the brain to think again
The soul to feel the flesh, and the flesh to feel the chain.[2]

At the same time it does not read like a made-up story. In apocryphal stories, like those included in the non-canonical Gospel of St. Thomas, we can read the kind of fantastic fable that is the result of invention: how, for instance, the boy Jesus made clay sparrows and then with one word "Fly!" endued them with life and power so that they flew over the housetops. Or we are

[2]Emily Brontë.

told that when pushed and jostled in the school playground by another lad, Jesus smote his playmate with leprosy. How different is this almost autoptic story, with its delineation of human grief, sublime faith, and the Master's supernatural power! A story of raising the *dead* might be made up and inserted in a book as late as the Fourth Gospel, but the details of human emotion are so lifelike as to argue strongly for historicity. We must leave the matter there.

Certainly it is highly unlikely that anyone would make up a sentence like "I am the Resurrection and the Life." And even if such a unique and humanly speaking preposterous sentence were invented, its meaning is substantiated by the glorious resurrection of Jesus himself from the dead.

Of all the events on which the white light of searching inquiry has been focused for centuries, there can hardly be one which has been so endlessly examined as the Resurrection. And it emerges triumphantly every time. One of our most brilliant lawyers set out to tear it to shreds and to publish an "exposure." All that he exposed was the unshakable nature of the evidence for it. The book ultimately published is, in my opinion, the finest apologetic for the Resurrection ever released from a press. Moreover, it is as exciting as a mystery thriller.[3]

What else but the fact of the Resurrection could have worked the greatest psychological miracle of all time, a miracle by which eleven depressed and terrified men, hiding in an upper room, "for fear of the Jews," were turned within six or seven weeks, to eleven heroic and courageous missionaries who openly proclaimed the Resurrection, which had transformed them, to audiences which included those who had plotted Christ's

[3] *Who Moved the Stone?* by Frank Morison.

death; men who had only to "produce the body" in order to silence the whole eleven, confound their faith, and strangle, almost at its birth, the Christian religion?

Of the *manner* of the Resurrection there is little yet to be said of value, though the field of psychic research may in time yield some suggestive clues which may help us to understand. Indeed, some theories have already been advanced.[4] But the early Christians did not bother about theories. Enough for them that, though in a different form, the same Jesus whom they had loved and followed had triumphantly survived death and had been able to convince them, beyond any shadow of doubt, that he was still alive and that death no longer had any dominion over him, or, save transitorily, over them either. Had he not spoken on preparing a place for them? And had not the greatest thinker among his followers declared that all the dead who had died "in Jesus," their Lord would gather to himself and "bring with him" (John 14:2; I Thess. 4:14).

We who have grown up, familiar all our lives with the accepted fact of the Resurrection and with at least some of its implications, cannot imagine what it must have meant to the earliest followers of Christ. To feel that hated Rome, with all her terrifying display of power, could not do anything more to the beloved and risen Savior, and to feel *that*, after feeling on the night of the Crucifixion that all was over like a beautiful dream that ends in a shattering awakening—this, I say, we cannot comprehend. But on top of that, to feel convinced, as they did, that no shadowy Hades, such as the rabbis had taught—and indeed such as the Old Testament still pictures—was theirs, but joyous and uninterrupted reunion with Christ and with their own loved ones—this

---

[4] I have discussed them in *His Life and Ours* (Abingdon Press), pp. 275 ff.

must have been wonder upon wonder. More wonderful even than that, in my opinion, was the conviction that the values he had taught and exemplified were established. The power of evil was shattered. It could not debase them. Rome, after all, was a passing evil. Permanence belonged to the Kingdom of love and truth and faith. Immortality came to *light* through the gospel. Where all had been dark, vague, shadowy, and unreal, the Resurrection put this earth-life in a completely new perspective. It gave meaning and purpose to events which otherwise seemed to point to an unjust or callous or blundering God.

Is it any wonder that the earliest preachers preached about Jesus and the Resurrection? Even at the risk of boring you, I want you to look at evidence that shows how the Resurrection, and the life it made possible, dominated the preaching of the early Church. Consider then the following passages:

With great power gave the apostles their witness of the resurrection of the Lord Jesus: and great grace was upon them all. (Acts 4:33)

[Paul] preached Jesus and the resurrection. (Acts. 17:18)

[At Athens] when they heard of the resurrection of the dead, some mocked. (Acts 17:32)

[Before Felix, Paul preached] a resurrection both of the just and unjust. (Acts 24:15)

If Christ hath not been raised, then is our preaching vain, your faith also is vain. . . . Ye are yet in your sins. Then they also which are fallen asleep in Christ have perished. If in this life only we have hoped in Christ, we are of all men most pitiable. But now hath Christ been raised from the dead. (I Cor. 15:14-20)

That ye may know . . . the exceeding greatness of his power to us-ward who believe, according to that working of the strength of his might which he wrought in Christ, when he raised him from the dead, and made him to sit at his right hand in the heavenly places, far above all rule, and authority, and power, and dominion, and every name that is named, not only in this world, but also in that which is to come. (Eph. 1:18-21)

That I may know him, and the power of his resurrection. (Phil. 3:10)

He ever liveth to make intercession for them. (Heb. 7:25)

The God of peace, who brought again from the dead the great shepherd of the sheep with the blood of the eternal covenant, even our Lord Jesus, make you perfect in every good thing to do his will, working in us that which is well-pleasing in his sight, through Jesus Christ; to whom be the glory for ever and ever. (Heb. 13:20)

Blessed be the God and Father of our Lord Jesus Christ, who according to his great mercy begat us again unto a living hope by the resurrection of Jesus Christ from the dead. (I Pet.1:3)

Finally, the last book of the Bible continually presents us with pictures of the Lamb that was slain, but who now is alive and reigning for evermore. "Behold," cries the risen Christ, "I am alive for evermore, and I have the keys of death and of Hades" (Rev. 1-18).

It is our modern custom to preach about the Resurrection on Easter Sunday each year, but I am sure we ought to speak about it far more than we do. On Easter is sounds like a nice happy ending to the sad story of Good Friday. It sounds also like comforting assurance to the bereaved that death is not the end. Further, it comforts us with an assurance of our own immortality. All these ideas are relevant and valuable, but I am sure they do not, either singly or together, explain the insistence on the Resurrection which the earliest preaching reveals and which the passages just quoted exemplify.

I would like to convey to you the *excitement* of a true appreciation of the Resurrection, by reading an oft-quoted passage from the life of one of our greatest preachers, R. W. Dale of Birmingham. He was preparing his sermons for Easter Sunday when the truth of the Resurrection suddenly seized him and thrilled him to the very soul. Later he wrote a passage in his diary which I am going to give to you, and every time he conducted a service thereafter, he included at least one hymn which contained the Resurrection message. Here is the passage:

"Christ is alive," I said to myself: "alive!" And then I paused: "Alive!" And then I paused again: "Alive!" Can that really be true? Living as really as I myself am? I got up and walked about repeating: "Christ is living! Christ is living!" At first it seemed strange and hardly true, but at last it came upon me as a burst of sudden glory; yes, Christ is alive. It was to me a new discovery. I thought that all along I had believed it; but not until that moment did I feel sure about it. I then said, "My people shall know it. I shall preach it again and again until they believe it as I do now."[5]

But I am bold to suggest to you that it was not merely the thought that Christ was still alive, and still able to commune with them and "manifest" himself to them, that produced the excitement of his disciples and gave birth to the emphasis in their subsequent teaching which we have noticed.

It is possible, though unlikely, that even if his body had remained visibly there in the tomb, subsequent generations might in time have made it a holy shrine, and some would doubtless have claimed to have communion with him, even as some people known to us claim to have communion with dear ones after death, even though their bodies be in a grave.

To put the matter another way, if, even now, proof were forthcoming that the physical body of Jesus had been found, the faith of the real Christian would not be

[5] A. W. Dale, *Life of R. W. Dale of Birmingham.*

destroyed, for he could not deny his religious experiences. He might interpret them differently, but he could hardly deny their validity, for his changed life would remain their monument.

I believe intensely in the fact of the physical Resurrection. Without the empty tomb, I cannot see that *so speedily* despair and fear would have been transformed into courage and heroism, but it seems illogical to me to suppose that the survival of Jesus depended on what happened to his body. Our own survival does not depend on what happens to our bodies, or on what happened to his, and apparently the survival of Elijah and Moses (Matt. 17:3; Mark 9:4; Luke 9:30), and possibly Samuel (I Sam. 28:13-15), did not necessitate their resurrection, for in the Bible record we meet them all long after their deaths.

What the empty tomb meant to the early Church was certainly an *immediate* assurance that Christ was alive, and that was of supreme importance to the infant faith of the Church. It meant also support for the faith that life goes on beyond the grave for all. For me, now, the puzzle of what happened to Christ's physical body—though extremely interesting—does not *matter* to my faith in the living Christ any more than the question of what happened to his clothes; or whence, for example, having been crucified practically naked, he obtained the clothes in which he appeared to Mary. His graveclothes remained in the tomb and were important evidence of his resurrection. In my opinion, the supreme value of the Resurrection was that it declared incontrovertibly that, by God's power, the mighty energies of a different and higher order or plane of being had invaded the earthly scene. The early Christians would not have expressed it thus, and perhaps it is enough to say that in the Resurrection God had spoken *from heaven*.

Let me try to elucidate this sentence. In an earlier

book, I defined a miracle not merely as something marvelous, but as

a law-abiding event by which God accomplishes His redemptive purposes through the release of energies which belong to a plane higher than any with which we are normally familiar.[6]

I want to keep the word "miracle" for events which demonstrate a breakthrough from a higher order.

An illustration is at hand from the way in which God made the world. We are told that at one time this earth was a mass of incandescent vapor. Through millions of years it gradually cooled. There must have been a time then, when every earthly landscape looked like the inside of a furnace. Nothing that we know of as life could possibly exist. No one looking on from outside could have predicted life. The setup, so to speak, on earth could not concoct life of itself. It was *all* of a nature inimical to life, namely red-hot matter. But life appeared. We know not how. Some think by radiation from some other planet or from a star. Into this I am not competent to enter, but it was the introjection from without the earth of energies which set up a new order called "life," energies which belonged to a higher order. A new era had begun.

In my view the Resurrection of Christ was similarly a new beginning through divine action taken from outside the circumstances. A new era began. Something happened that had never happened before and will never happen again—for it has no more *need* to happen again, any more than new created life need appear again. What has happened is enough for the divine purpose.

[6]*Psychology, Religion and Healing*, rev. (Abingdon Press).

I do not mean to imply, of course, that the early Church thought in this way, but they did realize that something tremendous had happened. God had acted in a new way as he had when he created life on a dead planet. Not only had the reality and power of the spiritual world been demonstrated, but its moral quality had been overwhelmingly demonstrated also, and the statement, "I am the Resurrection and the Life"—a statement substantiated by his resurrection—means in one sentence that Jesus opens up a new spiritual order. Death counts to the Christian as almost of no importance. It is only a gateway to fuller communion with Christ and with the blessed dead. Further, and much more important, evil has no significant power. It is all used and controlled by these higher forces of God which brought about the Resurrection of Christ. The lowly Christian virtues are authenticated, vindicated, and assured of permanent and final victory. They are the qualities in life that matter, for in the light of the Resurrection, the word "life" is not just biological existence functioning a planet. Man is primarily a spirit functioning in a spiritual universe so utterly marvelous and splendid that we can only make puerile guesses about it. All language falls baffled to the ground. In that universe such a being as Christ can manifest himself here and then eight miles away (Luke 24:13-16). He can talk and eat and yet pass through closed doors (Luke 24:36-43; John 20:19-25). If it is good for a man's faith, that man can touch a wounded side (John 20:24-29). If it is bad for a woman's faith to touch Him—imprisoning her in her senses from which He could otherwise set her free—then she must not touch Him (John 20:17).

Just as from the point of view of a dead and red-hot world, the growth of plants, the movements of fishes, the structure of a man, and the laughter of a child are incredible, so in a world in which resurrection can happen we may expect spiritual marvels, and the truth is we have scarcely made a beginning, because we are so slow to believe the passage that is before us, that he is Resurrection in a dead world, and he is "Life" with a connotation wider than we dare to dream.

This era which the Resurrection opened is not new merely because it led men to believe in survival after death. It supported such a faith, but devout men held it already. The Greeks and Romans did. The Hebrews did in a vague way. In the story before us, Martha says of her dead brother: "I know he will rise again." It is new because it manifests for the first time the use by God of powers belonging to another, and we may well say a *higher* plane of being, and it was a use in the cause of righteousness to the bewilderment and incipient defeat of evil. Power in high places, damnable and degrading tyrannies of monarchs and governments, world-rulers of darkness, even psychical principalities and powers, all were nullified and their final doom assured by the power which raised Jesus from the dead, and even if for a time evil simulated power and even success, yet goodness and love and truth were *established* and enthroned.

There was, by the resurrection of Jesus Christ from the dead, an inheritance, incorruptible, undefiled and that could never fade away, reserved in heaven for those who by the power of God had the insight to see and to live by this new revelation of God. The Christians of the first century were exhorted to rejoice. "Manifold temptations" remained, but their faith "more precious than gold" was proved. How privileged they were! Prophets had longed to see their words fulfilled and had been disappointed. Angels had desired to look into these things and been denied. And in their day God had spoken the most powerful word in history. And they, even they, had been allowed "in that dawn to be alive" (see I Pet. 1:3-12). The supernatural power of a holy, omnipotent God had burst forth again into history and geography, as it had done earlier on the first Christmas Day, and no life lived out on this earth in the future will ever be lived as if that event had never happened.

No wonder the early Christians were happy. They had watched this God-man closely until they could do no other than worship him. Monotheists though they were, they worshiped him, and, even more impressively, he accepted their worship as his right. Then, just when they were quite convinced that he was not as other men, then death seemed to prove that he was not big enough to vanquish it. It seemed that death could hold him like anybody else, that the power of the secular arm could finish with him as it finished with all reformers before him. No wonder they were shattered on Good Friday night! So this was the end! He could be put to death! This wonderful movement that sounded as though it were going to mark a new era was finished. Even he was subject to death. Calvary was the crucifixion of all their hopes as well as of their Master; of all their dreams as well as of their Lord. Then, on the third day, God, as it were, showed his hand. There was a supernatural energy at work behind all seeming. It was greater than death and greater than tyranny and greater than torture. They had suspicions of it before because Jesus said in the Garden: "Thinkest thou that I cannot now pray to my Father, and he shall send me more than twelve legions of angels?" Twelve legions of angels instead of twelve cowardly men! But the angels were held back at that point for the hour had not struck. The disciples had had suspicions when he worked his miracles that there were supernatural agencies at work. But nothing like this. This marked a new era and opened up a new world. "When Thou hadst overcome the sharpness of death Thou didst open the kingdom of heaven to all believers. Thou sittest at the right hand of God in the Glory of the Father."

Never again need we feel that evil can dominate the world and do what it likes with moral values. Here is their vindication. He is risen. As a friend of mine said, in a lovely sentence: "The goal of history has been kicked." To change the metaphor, all that remains are mopping-up operations. We are now certain of victory. We know now, without any doubt whatever, that if we believe in the Resurrection, evil can never win. The Lord God Omnipotent reigneth. When the apostles realized that, they felt this: "Well, others may walk still in a demon-haunted world, but not us. Others may fear death, but not us. Others may fear the secular arm, the power of the tyranny of Rome, but not us. He is risen. The new world is born. It has happened." Denial now would be as futile as trying to pluck the risen sun out of a summer sky and bring back to the light-gladdened earth the darkness of its midnight.

From all this two things flow for us. First, the joy that we ought to get as we contemplate the world. We all have dark and depressing moods when we forget the Resurrection. Things seem to be going from bad to worse. Governments come and go. We keep hoping, and then lose our optimism. We hear of evil and disaster and treachery and death. In people's homes there is strife, and between the nations there is distrust and suspicion and fear, and so often the apparent victory of evil. Remember Jesus Christ is risen from the dead. But for him I would sing another *Nunc Dimittis:* "Lord, lettest now thy servant depart in tears for mine eyes have seen hell." Two wars and another a possibility; fear spreading through the world; injustice rampant; what looks like culpable misunderstanding and stubborn intransigence preventing the nations from getting together. In every daily paper we read of horror and evil and disaster and sorrow and heartbreak. Unless there is a supernatural power that can do something; unless the hand of God is still on the helm of things, we are, of all men, most miserable, of all men most pitiable because we keep tying our hopes to something that continually proves itself utterly futile. But he is risen. The victory has been won. The powers of evil have been shattered. It has been proved that just behind all seeming there is a supernatural energy which, when the moment is right in the eyes of God, can break through and vindicate the faith of those who love and believe in him.

Second, this message brings joy to our own lives, for our own hearts are a microcosm of the macrocosm of the world. Who is there among us who, of his own will, has achieved the kind of victory he seeks? Now the Resurrection means victory in personal life. That is another thing that made those men so happy. They saw that sin was not the sort of thing that could eternally have power over them, leading them not only to constant defeat, but to constant despair about things. They felt that though sin is long a-dying and in its death throes can still do ugly things, yet it had received its mortal blow and could never recover its former strength.

James S. Stewart in one of his books has painted a picture which I should like to reproduce. I only wish I had his gift so that I could paint it for you as he does. It is the picture of the Upper Room before and after the Resurrection. If I may take the liberty of borrowing his illustration, I will use it a little differently, and imagine that you and I go to the Upper Room on the night of Calvary. We find the door is fast-barred for fear. We open it a little, but somebody says, "Shut that door!" for within, men are in terror. And when we squeeze ourselves in, we find a group of heartbroken, disillusioned, nervous, frightened men. Their faces are full of gloom. Their hearts are full of shame and darkness and despair. And we go away again. Then let us imagine that we go back on the night after the Resurrection, and we say to ourselves: "This can't be the house. It was all in darkness and it was shuttered up. This can't be the house. We must have got into the wrong street because the windows are open and men are singing and laughing." We go in, no one minds the door being opened now, and we are welcomed and we find the atmosphere is entirely different. Three words explain the difference. Jesus has risen.

Don't tell me that the Resurrection simply means that these men had become a little more sure that they could live again after death. They knew that before. What is the difference? He is alive and evil is beaten. So they went out from that new, changed, Upper Room because they knew that no power of death or hell or any form of evil could ever again hold the human race in everlasting bondage. Of course, we shall all be depressed and beaten sometimes. Temptation too often has its way with us, and we sin and then hate ourselves. The Devil, for a beaten foe, has the devil of a lot of kick left in him still! We think sometimes: "I shall never get where I want to be." But Jesus Christ is risen. Evil in our lives is beaten. There is a Companion now, if I could only make you realize it, that Risen Conquering One is nearer to you now than the person sitting next to you—always spiritually nearer to you than your dearest friend, and able to do for you more than you can ask or think.

Do you think the testimony of the saints is all neurotic illness and lies? When Livingstone says, "I go through the jungles of Africa and Jesus is by my side," is David Livingstone, the explorer, a neurotic patient? When

Samuel Rutherford writes from his cell in prison and says, "Jesus Christ came into my cell yesterday and every stone shone like a jewel," will you say— a bad case of hallucination? If so, you had better tear up the New Testament; you had better tear up all the lives of the saints. You can tear up the testimonies of people in every walk of life, in every country under heaven, and in every century since the Resurrection.

I was reading only recently, to refresh my mind, the story of Savonarola. You probably know it better than I. Savanarola was born almost exactly five hundred years ago, and was a bishop in the Roman Catholic Church and a mighty reformer. If only he had had his way, Roman Catholicism would not be today the intolerant and exclusive sect which now it is. A religion of freedom might have embraced the world. Savonarola had all Florence at his feet, and if it had not been for the Pope, he might have had all Italy. But, of course, the Pope fought him and appeared to win, for he took Savonarola, the saint, the mystic, and tortured him in ways that are too harrowing for description, until at last Savonarola was put to death. Just before he died, he said this: "They may kill me, they may tear me in pieces, but never, never, never shall they tear from my heart the living Christ."

Jesus said: "I am the resurrection, and the life: he that believeth on me, though he die, yet shall he live: and whosoever liveth and believeth on me shall never die."

XI

The Alpha and the Omega

I am the Alpha and the Omega, saith the Lord God, which is and which was and which is to come, the Almighty.
—REV. 1:8

THESE words are taken, as you perceive, from what we call the Apocalypse or The Revelation of St. John the Divine, and are in a different category from the other statements of Jesus which contain the words: "I am." The others, one feels, give us pictures of Christ which he has signed himself, though, of course, all of them come from another's reporting, and, indeed, when they reach our minds are in their third language, for Jesus spoke in Aramaic, was reported in Greek, and has been translated into English. Many of us like to get hold of a fourth edition and turn eagerly to Dr. Moffatt or J. B. Phillips!

The words "alpha" and "omega" denote, of course, the first and last letters of the Greek alphabet. The Authorized Version in some passages adds after the word "omega," the words "the beginning and the ending," and we might translate the passages: "I am the A and the Z."

This book, commonly called just Revelation, is one of great difficulty for modern English readers. If you get stuck in some parts of it, I am sure you are at liberty to comfort yourself with the solacing thought that there are some passages which no one understands! With all the puzzles left for the scholars to unravel, we will not concern ourselves. No one is sure who wrote the book.

There is some evidence that it was written by the author of the Fourth Gospel, but some scholars think that the style is so different and the references so obscure that it may not be by the same author at all. We are told that an obscure author might on occasion hide under the fame of a better-known name. The scholars disagree, and perhaps the question of who wrote it does not much matter. Some conclusions are really amusing. One large book, I am told, was written to prove that this book was not written by John, but by someone else of the same name!—an illuminating conclusion which does not help people like you and me very much. Another author proves in the first part of his volume that it may have been John the evangelist, and in the second that it may not have been he! When, having paid $3.50, we have read several hundred pages, we find that our author, as my friend Dr. Sangster would say, "has moved majestically from 'probably' to the more satisfying conclusion, 'probably not' "!

However, we must not laugh at the scholars, for we all owe them far too much. And they do seem agreed that the book was written between A.D. 81 and 93 during the reign of the Roman Emperor Domitian. It was he who recalled the whole Roman Empire to the practice of worshiping the emperor. Refusal to worship the emperor met with either exile or death. It is probable that the Christian writer of this strange book was exiled on the island of Patmos, off the coast of Greece, because he refused to worship the emperor.

Further, he is trying to write to his fellow Jewish Christians in such a way that he will be able to share with them his visions and his glorious certainties, and yet not incriminate them with the authorities. Many of his messages are doubtless in code. The "beast" may well be the emperor himself. The "scarlet woman" is thought to mean Rome, and so on. But at this distance of time and in our altered circumstances, we are as baffled when we read some parts of the book as anyone would be who is presented with a document written in code, but is not presented with the key. The result is that for honest Christians today the book is reminiscent of a pigeon pie with which my predecessor at the City Temple, Dr. Parker, was once regaled and which drew from him the comment: "Much pie, little pigeon!" Yet there is some good, nourishing meat if we search for it, and our text, repeated at least four times, is one of the most satisfying.

We can imagine our lonely visionary on his sea-girt island, longing for the voices of his fellow Christians and hearing only the crying of the gulls, the moan of the wind, and the fret of the sea. No wonder he writes: "And the sea is no more" (Rev. 21:1). The Jews have always hated the sea. They never have been a maritime race or done much business in great waters. The sea for them was the abode of evil spirits. It was a dreadful fate to be cast into the depths of the sea (Mark 9:42). Too many devils had been cast into it! (Mark 5:13). And to our author it symbolized not only evil, but separation and isolation from all that was most precious to him.

And yet not all: far from it, for as he came to meditate on Patmos he had a wonderful experience. He had slept little one night, and, lonely and depressed, had risen up before the dawn and wandered down to the seashore. Above him the stars flashed like gems in the splendor of the velvet night, at its darkest just before the dawn. It was early on the Lord's day and he longed to worship with those he had been compelled to leave. He turned toward Jerusalem, far in the east, and behold, the darkness was breaking. He had had his back to it, gazing mournfully at the black, hostile sea as yet unillumined by the dawn. But now the great splendor had begun. The color spread across the sky. Daffodil first with

141

gleams of pale green and primrose light, then the faintest pastel pink rapidly deepening to crimson and gold. John thought of the temple in Jerusalem catching the gleams in its golden dome as God's day of worship began. As a great wave crashed behind him on the beach, he turned at the noise and it seemed to shout to him, in a trumpet voice of majesty and assurance: "I am Alpha and Omega, the first and the last."

And now, as he faced west looking over the waters, the light of the rising sun behind him was glinting on the waves, lighting the whole scene. Before him, John seemed to see the vision of the Son of Man himself, magnified, majestic, immense. The paling stars seemed at his fingertips. The woolly, fleecy clouds at the zenith seemed to crown him with a supernatural purity. His eyes were flames of fire and his feet caught the yellow glory of the sunrise and shone like burnished brass. His countenance was radiant with sunshine and his voice mingled with the crashing breakers in front of him. John fell prostrate on the beach. His depression had vanished. He was "in the spirit on the Lord's day," as truly as if he had been in his beloved temple at Jerusalem, and his Master was as near to him. He seemed to feel a touch on his shoulder and that voice like many waters spoke the old familiar words which Jesus had used so often: "Fear not!"

Breathless now with adoration, John listened as the beloved inner Voice continued:

Fear not; I am the first and the last, and the Living one; and I was dead, and behold, I am alive for evermore, and I have the keys of death and of Hades. Write therefore the things which thou sawest, and the things which are, and the things which shall come to pass hereafter. (Rev. 1:17-19)

The message was complicated and it is now difficult to understand, but four times the words were repeated: "I am the Alpha and the Omega, the first and the last." Let us ask what they mean.

First of all, note how, by the time the seer is writing, the Christian religion claims as its own the whole universe of space, the whole range of time, past, present, and future, and every condition which the soul can reach, for Christ has the keys of death and the whole world of the spirit.

The alpha of it is lost in the mystery of the Eternal Son. The beta of it was a young Man teaching and healing by the lakeside. The gamma of it was a Hero crucified and risen. But these, impressive and beautiful though they were, comprised but the A B C of his significance. That significance, John realized in his visions, went on through a score of ever-mounting grades and levels.

This very amazing claim that is made for what we now call "the cosmic Christ" stands out a little more clearly when we realize what has happened in other religions. No such claims have ever been made elsewhere. For example, nothing was written down about the Buddha until more than five hundred years after his death. But even now he is not *worshiped*. He is still regarded as what he was, a very wise and saintly human teacher, an avatar, who found and practiced a beautiful and unselfish way of life which he believed would lead to a wonderful and rich experience in some future state. I imagine a Buddhist would laugh at you if you asked whether Buddha had any hand in the creation of the world. Buddha himself was an atheist.[1]

Whatever point our own Christian thought and belief may have reached, we must acknowledge an amazing thing. By A.D. 90 the Christians had put Christ on the

[1]Prayer was not advocated in Buddhism until long after the Buddha's death. One of the leading Buddhists in London said to me: "Don't use the Word 'God'; it has no meaning at all for me or my fellow Buddhists."

throne of God. Monotheists to a man, like all good Jews, they worshiped him. They regarded him as equal with God. They hailed him as King of kings, as Lord of lords, as the one in whom the universe held together, and—above all in this book of Revelation—the one who would speedily come as Vindicator and Judge. The incarnation was heralded by Bethlehem's angels. The consummation would mean the universe rolled up and the Saviour the crowned King of every created soul.

Listen to some of the language and ask whether words can describe any greater exaltation.

In the beginning was the Word, and the Word was with God and the Word was God. . . . All things were made by him; and without him was not anything made that hath been made. In him was life; and the life was the light of men. (John 1:1-4)

Listen to Paul talking to the Ephesians of the power of God in Christ,

when he raised him from the dead, and made him to sit at his right hand in the heavenly places, far above all rule, and authority, and power, and dominion, and every name that is named, not only in this world, but also in that which is to come: and he put all things in subjection under his feet, and gave him to be head over all things to the church, which is his body, the fulness of him that filleth all in all. (Eph. 1:20-23)

Listen to the famous passage to the Philippian Christians about the Christ,

who, being in the form of God, counted it not a prize to be on an equality with God, but emptied himself, taking the form of a servant, being made in the likeness of men: and being found in fashion as a man, he humbled himself, becoming obedient even unto death, yea, the death of the cross. Wherefore also God highly exalted him, and gave unto him the name which is above every name; that in the name of Jesus every knee should bow, of things in heaven and things on earth and things under the earth, and that every tongue should confess that Jesus Christ is Lord, to the glory of God the Father. (Phil. 2:6-11)

Listen to similar words addressed to the Colossians. He says of Christ, he

is the image of the invisible God, the firstborn of all creation; for in him were all things created, in the heavens and upon the earth, things visible and things invisible, whether thrones or dominions or principalities or powers; all things have been created through him and unto him; and he is before all things, and in him all things consist [= hold together]. And he is the head of the body, the church: who is the beginning, the firstborn from the dead; that in all things he might have the pre-eminence. For it was the good pleasure of the Father that in him should all the fulness dwell; and through him to reconcile all things unto himself, having made peace through the blood of his cross; through him, I say, whether things upon the earth, or things in the heavens. (Col. 1:15-20)

Bernard Shaw called the book of Revelation "the ravings of a drug-addict," but quite plainly and quite independently Paul made earlier the same cosmic claims for Christ. From that humble birth, we proceed in the New Testament to the point where Christ is worshiped and adored as God, the one who makes sense of all things in heaven and earth, the one who was the Creative Principle in the beginning and will bring about the final climax at the end of history.

All this is not pompous oriental imagery without relevance for today. The world often looks as if it has gone astray. Man's heart trembles for fear at the very discoveries of power which he himself has made. Belief in God seems often on the wane and men wonder what the end will be. The Christian message is that the climax of history will be worthy of the Creator, that a strong hand is in control, that the string of events we call history will not end in meaninglessness, or run out like a stream that loses itself in the desert, but that Christ will reign and his promise be fulfilled: "Heaven and earth shall pass away: but my words shall not pass away" (Mark 13:31); for "the Lord our God, the Almighty, reigneth" (Rev. 19:6).

Men naturally ask questions at this point. Will Christ visibly return to earth and reign? Will the kingdom come on earth or in some future heaven? What will the omega, the end, be like?

Let us take the questions in reverse order and try to answer them. To the last I have only the briefest answer. No one can possibly know. All that one can be sure about is that the final winding-up of the human story will be worthy of the nature of God and the sacrificing love of the Redeemer. No one could rest his mind in Mark Twain's cynical conclusion that "human history is a rather discreditable episode in a drama of one of the minor planets." If the Son of God takes a rôle in the drama the play forthwith takes on a divine significance.

Will the kingdom come on earth? I am one of those who believe that the answer to this question is yes, though many, for whom I have a profound regard, do not believe this. They think that on some other plane the consummation of history will occur. For myself, however, it seems odd that Christ should teach men in the model prayer to pray, "Thy kingdom come, thy will be done *on earth* as it is in heaven," if, in fact, the prayer will never be answered. I admit that the intransigence of man makes possible the temporary defeat of God. Yet John himself, with other scriptural seers, saw in their visions not only a new heaven, but a new earth (Rev. 21:1; cf. Rev. 5:13; II Pet. 3:13; Hab. 2:14), and the Bethlehem angels promised peace *on earth* among the men of good will.

As I complete this book, men are engaged in building

the new City Temple. The plans of our excellent architects have been approved and the work is proceeding. I should be very surprised if one day the architects told me that they were very sorry but their plans could not be worked out on that site, with the material they had gathered, because the workmen were hopelessly incapable, and that they now suggested trying on another site with different material and better workmen.

It seems to me that the Great Architect of the Universe has a plan to build what we often call the City of God here on this earth. The faithful among his workmen have labored—often with little enough sight of the plans—for two thousand years so that the Architect's plans might be worked out in a happier and more blessed order. Has God lost faith in his workmen? Or are the plans impracticable? If so, didn't he know that at the beginning? What should we think of an architect who knew, before he employed the contractors, that the building would never be finished? Why all the blood and sweat and tears of the missionaries, the saints and martyrs, if the dream of a happy earth, with all men joined in a great family of brothers, living a life of fellowship and sharing "all the blessings of this life," is only a dream from which we shall all awaken to the somber actuality of some lower reality? It would seem to me to be a poor substitute to remove the site to some heavenly sphere and employ angelic workmen to translate the dream into the reality of a fellowship of spirits in heaven.

As to the other question, whether Christ will visibly return to earth and reign, I am not one who believes that the visible form of a man will descend literally from the clouds. Ask yourself just what that would accomplish. Would he reign? Would he not be hurried to a mental hospital? How could such a local return influence the whole world? To me the question has a ludicrous side. Would the returning Messiah be dressed like Gandhi, or descend in the West in a natty blue suit and a bowler hat?

I have dealt with this matter very fully elsewhere[2] and will only say briefly here three things.

1. Many of the promises Christ made about his return were fulfilled when he came in the Spirit at Pentecost (e.g., Matt. 16:28; 10:23; 24:30).

2. If it be supposed that his return will be accompanied by supernatural "fireworks," can we really think that if love fails to win men, terror and overwhelming force will accomplish a divine aim? Has he who repudiated force and fear changed his nature?

3. At the same time I sincerely accept what I think the Second Adventist is trying to establish; namely, that Christ will not be defeated, love will not go unvindicated, eternal values will be proved the real values, and this lovely earth, which under God's hand produced the amazing creature we call man, will see man redeemed.

Christ, having begun a great work, will not throw it up in despair, but complete it (Phil. 1:6). "He shall see of the travail of his soul, and shall be satisfied" (Isa. 53:11). When all men love him and serve him by serving one another; when all live in a global family using all scientific discovery for brotherly purposes; when the assets of one are shared by all and the sorrows of one are the concern of all; when "nation shall not lift up sword against nation, neither shall they learn war anymore" (Isa.2:4), then indeed Christ will have *come* in a sense far more true and far more significant and valuable than any literal appearance of an individual in the literal clouds. I can conceive no more worthy climax to human history, no more impressive Second Advent than that.

[2]*When the Lamp Flickers* (Abingdon Press), Ch. 17, "Will Christ Visibly Return to Earth?" pp. 165 ff.

Jesus shall reign where'er the sun
Doth his successive journeys run;
His kingdom stretch from shore to shore,
Till suns shall rise and set no more.

In this faith the faithful in the Church on earth labor on in the face of indifference, abuse, and scorn. If all turns out as the Christian believes, how intensely some will wish they had joined in the fight earlier. We all know that in the hour of triumph no cause lacks supporters. Yet it probably will not avail much to say to God, "I didn't join the church, it is true, but I had an aunt who was a big Baptist"! One recalls the famous words of the French Henry IV to the cowardly Crillon after the battle of Arques: "Hang yourself, brave Crillon; we fought at Arques and you were not there!"

By faith the Christian sees the omega of the Christian battle and he rejoices to hasten its certain victory.

Our theme seems relevant today in two ways, first a comforting and second, a challenging way.

l. Lately a woman I know married at forty years of age. She was good enough to talk to me very frankly. On her own showing she had grown sarcastic and cynical. She had said many bitter things about many better folk than herself. She had envied their good luck in being married and having their own homes. She had secretly wept many tears of frustration. She had ceased praying years ago and thought God, if he existed, had given her a very poor deal in life. Then, rather late, love came into her life. A youngish widower claimed and won her. She was radiant, a different creature, full of love for others and laughter and joy. Her whole being, she said, was transformed. Then she added this most significant, if unfinished, sentence: "If only I had known earlier how life was going to turn out—" She meant she would not have said some of the cutting, sarcastic things with which she had wounded others. She would have been easier to live with and much happier.

I do not write this in any critical spirit. I know only too poignantly my own failures; how different life would have been if at the point Alpha I had known the Omega.

How one admires the great spirits who went out "not knowing whither they went." Men praise Abraham, the great patriarch and father of a nation, for they look *back* upon his grave venture of faith, but what about his feelings a hundred miles out of Ur in the frightful and horrific loneliness of the vast and pitiless desert? We praise Moses now for showing the wisdom of a great statesman and lawgiver, the tactics of a great general, the piety of a saint, but to guide the rabble of Israel through the wilderness for forty years and hold together those nomad tribes until they became something like a nation demanded courage and greatness beyond computation.

When Moses felt the pains of death coming upon him, ordering that none should follow him, like another gallant gentleman, he too walked out into the snow. Otherwise his tomb would have been made a shrine and his devotees, tarrying by a grave, would have failed to make progress toward the promised land. Climbing up to the snow-clad heights of Nebo, he lay down to die and "no man knoweth his sepulchre until this day." If only he could have known how it would all end!

The message of our theme is that to some extent the end is known by faith. Perhaps in regard to Moses the author of the letter to the Hebrews disclosed the secret when he wrote: "He endured as seeing him who is invisible."

It is part of our schooling here on earth that we may not know the detail of the end of our story. But because Christ is the Omega, the end of the story will be worthy of him. We are in the hands of one, infinitely wise and loving and ultimately omnipotent, who will bring every story to a fitting climax if we walk humbly and trust him and live a day at a time. "We bring our years to an end as a tale that is told," but it will be a good story, with a moral, a purpose, and a satisfying end.

Of course, this does not mean that from our point of view every life will achieve its ambition. We think of Captain Scott perishing only eleven miles from safety. Yet at the end he did not whine. He wrote: "How much better it has been than lounging in too great comfort at home!" And again, in his diary we find these words: "I do not regret this journey which has shown that Englishmen can endure hardness, help one another, and meet death with as great a fortitude as ever in the past."[3]

I believe that from Alpha to Omega we are in the hands of that wise, loving, omnipotent, disciplinarian Father whom we call God, and that when Omega is reached we shall all sincerely say: "I do not regret this journey." I recall a verse from my father's favorite hymn:

> With mercy and with judgement
>   My web of time He wove,
> And aye the dews of sorrow
>   Were lustred by His love,
> I'll bless the hand that guided,
>   I'll bless the heart that planned,
> When throned where glory dwelleth
>   In Immanuel's land.

There is no sorrow, no pain, no frustration, no grief, which he cannot weave into his pattern, though its threads may have been spun by evil, ignorant, or foolish

---

[3]Captain E. R. G. R. Evans, *South with Scott.*

hands, and when the whole pattern is spread before our eyes, we shall have no complaints. Marveling at the Weaver's skill, we shall say: "It is the Lord's doing and it is marvelous in our eyes."

2. But there is challenge as well as comfort in this thought. Paul wrote down a very wonderful sentence when he said; "To me to live is Christ." If I may translate that verse a little differently, it would be with Dr. Moffatt thus: "Life means Christ to me" (Phil. 1:21). We could translate, "Jesus is the A to Z of living." I wonder if we are anywhere near being able to say that; I am quite sure it should be true for every one of us. This modern life, which you and I have to live today, tomorrow, and the next day, has no real meaning apart from Christ. He is the A to Z of its meaning. Apart from him, who by his own life has given it meaning and purpose and beauty, it has no joy, no satisfaction, no goal, no worthwhileness at all. I am quite sure that all pathways that lead away from him lead either to illness of body or mind, or to a dreadful sense of meaninglessness and frustration, or to complete moral disaster, or else to that awful stupefied groping which we find sometimes in elderly people who in the eventide of life, having ignored real religion, are found looking for an interpretation of life that makes sense, looking for a philosophy of life that lifts them out of monotony and gray, killing boredom, looking for a path that will bring them somewhere worth getting.

It is rather a grim thing to say, but I think in the light of our theme we have to say it. *Jesus is inescapable.* He who stood at the beginning of your journey is standing at the end of the path you are on now. H stands at the end of Everyman's path. You cannot evade him. You cannot cut across the fields. You have to keep on the road of your life, and he is standing at the end of it, and if you do not meet him as Saviour, you will confront him as Judge. Every eye shall see him. "They shall look on him whom they have pierced." He who is Alpha is Omega too, and cannot be evaded, or side-stepped, or escaped. How wise we should be to anticipate that inevitable encounter! How wise we should be to make him the Alpha and the Omega of every day, so that waking we offer to him our day, so that sleeping we say, "Into thy hands I commend my spirit"!

In the summer of 1955, I completed forty years in the Methodist ministry. If any should say to me, "What lesson have you most clearly learned in that time?" I know without the hesitation of a second what my answer would be. It would be that life will only work out one way and that is God's way. All other ways are either "dead ends" from which one must turn back and try again, or else they lead to a precipice. "Outside God there is only death." Never forget that. Life was made for God. An automobile is made for roads. If you drive it into a swamp or a ditch, well, it will stop. It was not created for that purpose. You must drag it back on the road again. God grant you don't smash it up through your driving, or drive over the cliffs before you can pull up. If I try to use my life only for pleasure, or gain, or lust, or any form of selfishness, then life just breaks down. It was not created for that purpose. Illness of body or mind, frustration, boredom, irritability, or depression warn us that life was made for God, not for us, save as we offer him our lives and cooperate in his plans. "Thou hast made us for thyself."

Listen to one whose teaching has always profoundly helped me.

The very secret of all profitable use of life is just to abandon the expectation that it ever was designed to forward persons devoted to material and merely worldly purposes, with no higher ends than gain or pleasure or pride of place, and to discern that naturally the only ends it could have been designed to serve are God's.[4]

Whatever road you may be on, Jesus Christ confronts you from A to Z. He is willing to be the Friend, the Companion, the Sustainer, the Guide, the Saviour. But if you refuse he still remains the King and the Judge. I am not trying to frighten you. In any case no man can be frightened into the love-relationship with Christ which is the heart of Christianity. I am not suggesting a lurid judgment day or hinting at the flames of hell. I am stating what I believe is a fact of the gravest importance, namely that Jesus Christ is someone with whom sooner or later we shall all have to do.[5] We may not need to worry about a literal appearance before a literal throne or judgment seat of Christ. But we shall find some encounter with him inescapable. As the Cockney soldier said:

> There ain't no throne, and there ain't no
>   books,
>   It's 'Im you've got to see,
> It's 'Im, just 'Im, that is the Judge
>   Of blokes like you and me.
> And, boys, I'd sooner frizzle up,
>   I' the flames of a burnin' 'Ell,
> Than stand and look into 'Is face,
>   And 'ear 'Is voice say—*"Well?"*[6]

When the dread moment comes, how miserably ashamed we shall be that we missed the path that would

[4]Dr. John Oman, *Paradox of the World.*
[5]"There is no creature that is not manifest in his sight: but all things are naked and laid open before the eyes of him with whom we have to do." (Heb. 4:13)
[6]From "Well?" by G. A. Studdert-Kennedy, in *The Unutterable Beauty* © 1927 and reprinted by permission of Hodder & Stoughton Limited.

have led to peace and joy and integration. If you meet him now and accept his offer of friendship, how wise, how very, very wise you will be!

If I had to express the heart of the gospel in one sentence it would be this: Christ offers his friendship to you.

> Yea thro' life, death, thro' sorrow and thro' sinning
> He shall suffice me, for he hath sufficed:
> Christ is the end, for Christ was the beginning,
> Christ the beginning, for the end is Christ.[7]

[7] F. W. H. Myers, *St. Paul.*